CHEW
THIS JOURNAL

CHEW
THIS JOURNAL

An Activity Book for You and Your Dog

SASSAFRAS LOWREY

mango
PUBLISHING GROUP

CORAL GABLES

Cover Design: Elina Diaz
Cover Photo/illustration: shutterstock.com/GooseFrol
Layout & Design: Elina Diaz

For permission requests, please contact the publisher at:
Mango Publishing Group
2850 S Douglas Road, 2nd Floor
Coral Gables, FL 33134 USA
info@mango.bz

For special orders, quantity sales, course adoptions and corporate sales, please email the publisher at sales@mango.bz. For trade and wholesale sales, please contact Ingram Publisher Services at customer.service@ingramcontent.com or +1.800.509.4887.

Chew This Journal: An Activity Book for You and Your Dog

Library of Congress Cataloging-in-Publication number: 2020934388
ISBN: (print) 978-1-64250-273-2, (ebook) 978-1-64250-274-9
BISAC category code: PET004020—PETS / Dogs / Training

Printed in the United States of America

*In memory of Charlotte
and for all of my dogs, past and present.*

TABLE OF CONTENTS

FOREWORD

Taking part in joint activities can strengthen the bond between a person and their dog, and providing enrichment is good for dogs' mental well-being. Chew This Journal fits perfectly with the increasing trend for providing enrichment for dogs. It combines fun challenges to do with your dog, craft activities, and plenty of space to journal about your best friend.

As in hir book Tricks in the City: For Daring Dogs and the Humans that Love Them, Sassafras Lowrey has considered the individual needs of different dogs and tried to ensure that activities are suitable for all, including senior dogs and shy dogs. For example, in the section on teaching your dog to jump, Lowrey explains that you should get clearance from your vet in order to protect your dog's joints. This thoughtfulness means Chew This Journal is appropriate for people with dogs of all sizes, ages, and personalities. Whether it's the walk-a-day challenge, the sniff walk, or building dog tunnels in your living room, there are many enjoyable activities for your furry friend in this book. As a certified trick-dog instructor, Lowrey has broken the more complicated tricks and sports down into easy-to-achieve steps.

I was especially pleased to see the inclusion of "Learn Their Names," as this was a fun activity that I used to enjoy with my late dog, Bodger. In the last two years of his life, we started to teach him the names of his toys—rope, bear, sheep, hog, turtle—and ask him to fetch them by name. He wasn't a genius, but it brought him a lot of joy. I think Bodger would have been a fan of this book.

Chew This Journal is not just about activities for dogs, however. There are some fun canine-inspired activities, especially if you like crafts. There's no need to buy snuffle mats and tug toys from the store when you can make your own. The ideas for photo props are cute and I think will result in pet guardians sharing photos of their dog and tagging the book!

Good dog owners are good neighbors, and Lowrey includes notes to help you be a good neighbor whilst taking part in the activities, such as keeping your dog on leash in on-leash areas. There is a section on giving back to local organizations such as shelters and rescue homes, pet food banks, or groups that help the pets of the homeless. There are also instructions on how to make an emergency kit for your dog—something all dog owners should have, just in case. Lowrey has thought carefully about how dog guardians can be good citizens and responsible pet parents.

This delightful book will bring joy to you and your dog. It will inspire you to try new activities together and to keep the journal as a treasured record of life with your pet. It's a book that's designed to be used—not chewed (or at least not too much), but certainly written in, doodled in, and taken out and about when planning to do some of the activities. And it's a book to return to over time, to update and keep track of what you and your dog have been up to. I think you will enjoy it, and you and your dog will have lots of fun.

Zazie Todd, PhD
Author of *Wag: The Science of Making Your Dog Happy* and blogger at
CompanionAnimalPsychology.com

INTRODUCTION

My earliest childhood memories revolve around dogs: dreaming of them, learning about them, and eventually, when I got a dog of my own, finding ways to have fun together. As a teenager, I began channeling my infatuation for dogs into training and competing in the sport of dog agility. I have learned far more from dogs than I have taught them. The greatest joy in my life is spending time with my dogs and having the opportunity to learn with them. I believe that dogs not only make my life more interesting, they truly make me a more thoughtful, mindful, and engaged person. As a certified trick-dog instructor (CTDI), I see it as one of my missions in life to support dogs in getting the opportunities to have more fulfilled and enriching lives by doing things that they love. Part of this is assisting people to better understand, support, advocate for, and engage with their dogs.

For me, training dogs isn't about telling them what to do; rather, it's about developing a channel for pet owner and dog to communicate with each other. Much more important to me than any ribbon, title, or award has and continues to be the deep pleasure in spending time with dogs, having fun together, and developing new paths of shared understanding and language. Several years ago, I began practicing goal setting, bullet journaling, and memory keeping on paper as a way to remember, structure, and organize my training and adventures with my dogs. This practice has enabled me to keep track of the fun things we do together, and to track progress toward the goals we set; practical training and grooming goals as well as exercise, travel, and even bucket lists and vacations. I have tried to incorporate into this book easy step-by-step ideas for introducing those same simple journaling/tracking techniques into your routine, as well as many of the same training and activity challenges my dogs and I regularly do. I have a three-year-old Newfoundland who is over a hundred pounds, and a ten-pound, seventeen-year-old Chihuahua mix. Having dogs of such radically different sizes and ages made me very aware of how important it was to select activities for this book that are appropriate and accessible for dogs of a wide range of abilities.

This book is filled with crafts, games, puzzles, and other opportunities for you to keep memories of what makes your dog special and unique! The world can sometimes feel like an overwhelming, confusing place, but dogs help us see the joy in simple, everyday moments. If you are reading this book, you probably love dogs just as much as I do. These activities are some of my dogs' favorite things, and we are thrilled to share these adventures with all of you. I hope Chew This Journal will inspire you to find new ways to connect, play, and spend intentional time with your dog!

Sassafras, Mercury, & Sirius

HOW TO USE THIS BOOK

This activity book belongs to you and your dog! Despite the name, I would encourage you not to allow your dog to literally chew on the book. I'm not a vet, but I can say it probably wouldn't be very good for them. Beyond that though, there is no wrong way to use this book. You can go through the activities in order, or you can open to a random page, do that activity, and jump around between different ones that interest you. This book is designed for you to write in, and is interactive, so don't be afraid to personalize it! My hope is that you will make the book your own: break the spine, doodle, take notes, paste in pictures... There is no wrong way to use this book so long as you and your dog are having fun.

Dogs never worry about being good at something, they are (for the most part) up for trying anything and everything. Dogs don't fret about messing up; to them, everything is a game. Try to take after dogs when you explore the activities in this book. Don't worry about being good at something, just have fun! As you go through this book, do whatever activities stand out to you and sound fun for you and your dog on a given day. Jump around, you do not need to do each activity in order. Most of all, have fun and challenge yourself and your dog to spend time together exploring something new! The idea behind this book is to support you and your dog having more fun together. It's about creating habits of enrichment where you two build routines together through different challenges and activities, and encouraging you to spend time thinking about how you want to spend time intentionally with your dog.

These activities are also about finding what your dog will and won't enjoy, and doing more of the former and less of the latter. There are already so many things that we control in our dogs' daily lives, things that they do because we need them to for safety reasons or because of our lifestyle. When we are focusing on doing enriching activities together, I think it's important that our dogs have a lot of input into what we do and don't do. If there's an activity that isn't fun for you, don't do it! Similarly, if there is an activity that you really like but your dog is ambivalent about or outright dislikes, I would encourage you to skip it. For example, I really enjoy the sport of Rally Obedience—it's sort of like traditional obedience but with a whole lot of fun and enthusiasm injected into it. I find it fun and challenging and it scratches a lot of the itching I felt being a former dog-agility competitor: I know how to build drive and enthusiasm in my dog and how to make activities and training sessions fun. I trained my youngest dog, Sirius, a lot in Rally. We even competed, and what I learned was that I don't want to do a sport my dog is only doing because I'm asking her to. Tricks? Sirius loves tricks and she excels at them. She's actually only the second Newfoundland in the world to earn her Champion Trick Dog title! So with her, I do a lot more tricks and skip the obedience ring. Taking this approach to dog activities can be hard, and it flies in the face of a lot of what we might historically have been socialized to think about the human-dog relationship, which privileges what people want over dogs. I believe our dogs deserve a better and more evolved approach. They deserve to spend time doing activities that are enjoyable for them.

Set yourself up for success with these activities. Not all dogs are the same and not all have the same interests or capacities, and that's ok; there will be lots of activities in this book that your dog can do. Life for the modern dog is hard! In some ways, many of today's canines are very privileged compared to those of only a few decades ago. Our dogs have veterinary specialists, high-quality food, and a plethora of toys. But there are also challenges to being a dog today. The current expectations we have for them, from their behavior in the home to out in the world, is intense. Dogs are not stuffed animals, yet increasingly in our culture they are expected to behave like they are. Too frequently dogs are expected to be seen and not heard, to be willing and happy to meet large groups of new people or dogs. I believe that living more intentionally with our dogs means not seeing them as accessories, property, or sports equipment to take out when it's convenient for us. Instead, in this book, we're going to do activities with our dogs that enrich their lives, and I hope that this book will inspire you to add games and intentional fun to your dog's life.

TIPS FOR GETTING STARTED

GOOD NEIGHBORS

Some of the activities in this book will have you and your dog going out into the world exploring your neighborhood, local parks, and beyond! I love going places with my dogs and giving them as enriching a life as possible, and want to inspire you to get out and exploring with your dog as well. However, as you are engaging with your pet in the world, it's important to remember to always be a good neighbor—to follow leash laws, pick up poop, and keep your dog close to you. All outdoor activities in this book can be done with your dog on a regular six-foot leash. Even if your dog is extremely friendly, not every dog or person in public will feel comfortable engaging with them, and that's ok! By respecting leash laws, not only are you keeping your dog safe, you are also supporting more areas remaining dog friendly!

TREATS

The activities in this book are designed to be as accessible as possible so you won't need a lot of props or supplies. One thing you will need, however, is treats! It's important to make sure that you are "paying" your dog for a job well done if they are performing tricks or learning a new game. There are people who get very caught up in the idea that they want their dog to enjoy doing things with them and don't want to feel like they are "bribing" their dogs to engage, or who say they only want their dog to be rewarded by praise. Even if you love your job (and dogs, generally speaking, love the sports and games they participate in), you wouldn't be too happy if you were paid in praise. Sure, it feels good to be told you did a good job, but you probably also want to see some money in your bank account. Dogs are the same way, only they don't want paychecks, they would much prefer string cheese and hotdogs!

By treating our dogs, we are able to communicate to them that they are doing a great job. We aren't bribing our dogs; rather, we are compensating them for a job well done. Just like us, different dogs have different taste preferences. Take some time to experiment with what kinds of treats your dog will eat, what your dog likes, and what your dog loves. As you play and train with your dog, you'll be paying them in the currency that matters most to them. For some dogs, this will mean playing with toys, especially games like tug, and most dogs, in addition to play, will feel highly rewarded by food. You will probably need to do a little bit of trial and error to figure out what sorts of treats your dog likes and how much they like them. The goal is to have different levels of reward—things your dog will eat and enjoy; things your dog really likes; and things your dog loves and would do anything to get. This last category will be our "high value" treat, which you will use especially when you are teaching your dog something new and challenging or upping the criteria, like trying to do a complicated skill in a new or more distracting environment.

Try different treats with your dog: commercially available treats all work well. You might also try bits of meat, hotdogs, cubes of cheese, or string cheese. Record your dog's reactions below, building a hierarchy of treats so you know what your dog will eat, what they really like, and what your dog loves. Again, anything in the love category, the "high value" treats, you should use for teaching new behaviors and practicing challenging skills.

EATS	LIKES	LOVES

TRAINING APPROACHES

I try to keep the activities in this book as simplistic as possible, and as often as possible to base them around household props and supplies that you likely already have available to you or that you can make, find, borrow, or purchase inexpensively. The most important thing is spending time with our dogs, learning from them as much as they are learning from us, and we don't need fancy equipment for that. Some of these activities are designed for you and your dog to do at home, and for other activities you and your dog will need to get out and explore the world together. Be sure your dog is walking with a properly fitted flat-buckle collar, harness, or a head halter. Never use any kind of equipment that is designed to cause pain such as slip/choke chains, prong collars, or shock collars. Pain should not be part of training and playing with our dogs.

THE DOG IS NEVER WRONG—DON'T PUNISH

As you and your dog are enjoying these activities and games, remember there is no way for your dog to be wrong. If we are working on an activity or game and our dog doesn't do what we are hoping or anticipating they will do, our dog isn't wrong, it simply means we haven't set up the situation for them to be successful. Usually, we have moved too quickly, have upped the criteria beyond what our dog is able to follow, there are too many distractions, or the activity is just too hard right now. In these moments, it's on us to shift the criteria so that our dog is able to be successful.

All training you do with your dog should be based on positive reinforcement: reward and praise. No dogs, regardless of their breed or size, need "a firm hand" or to be "shown who is boss." These intimidations or pain-based approaches to training are the kind that a lot of us grew up witnessing or learning. What we know now, thanks to a whole lot of research and science, is that this kind of training is actually really detrimental to dogs and their ability to trust, as well as their mental well-being and capacity to learn. Dogs need consistency, kindness, patience, and dedication from us.

WHAT KIND OF DOG TRAINING HAVE YOU PREVIOUSLY DONE?

_____

_____

_____

_____

WHAT WAS YOUR APPROACH?

_____

_____

_____

WHAT KIND OF A TRAINING RELATIONSHIP DO YOU WANT TO HAVE WITH YOUR DOG?

_____

_____

_____

SAFETY

The vast majority of the activities in this book are low impact and are going to be safe for dogs of all sizes and ages. With that said, always talk to your vet beforehand if you are uncertain about your dog's capacity to train or engage in activities. This is especially important for elderly dogs and young puppies. Dogs' joints are very fragile as they are developing and growing. The larger your dog is, the longer it will take for them to be fully grown and developed. For giant dogs, this might mean fifteen to eighteen months.

ACTIVITIES

FAVORITE TOYS

Plush toys, squeaky toys, grunting toys, rope toys; there are so many options! Most dogs have a variety of toys to choose from, and like little kids, they all have their favorites. Maybe it's the toy they carry around, or one they always bring to you to throw. What are your dog's favorite toys? Favorite toys can even change over time, so it's fun to periodically come back and review/update how your dog's preferences have changed!

DATE:

FAVORITE TOYS:

_____

_____

_____

_____

DATE:

FAVORITE TOYS:

_____

_____

_____

_____

DATE:

FAVORITE TOYS:

_____

_____

_____

_____

DATE:

FAVORITE TOYS:

_____

_____

_____

_____

DATE:

FAVORITE TOYS:

_____

_____

_____

_____

ABOUT MY DOG

1. My dog's birthday/gotcha day is: _____

2. My dog and I met
    (where/when): _____

3. My dog's breed or mix of breeds is: _____

4. My dog's favorite treat is: _____

5. My dog loves it when: _____

6. If my dog was a person their job would be: _____

7. My dog's favorite person is: _____

8. My dog's favorite toy is: _____

9. My dog likes to go to: _____

10. My dog's worst habit is: _____

11. My dog is scared of: _____

12. My dog's best friend is: _____

13. The funniest thing about my dog is: _____

14. My dog's favorite game is: _____

FIRST MEETING

Do you remember the very first moment that you met your dog?
Did you see his face on your computer screen and know that he was meant to be in your life?
Were you following her growth from ultrasound pictures, or did you meet him at an adoption
event? There are no wrong ways to meet your beloved best canine friend for the first time!
For most of us the moment we first met our dog will never leave our mind!

WRITE THE STORY OF HOW YOU FIRST MET YOUR DOG.

_____

_____

_____

_____

WHERE DID YOU MEET?

_____

_____

_____

WHAT WAS YOUR DOG LIKE?

_____

_____

WHAT WAS YOUR FAVORITE THING ABOUT YOUR DOG WHEN YOU MET?

WAS THERE ANYTHING ABOUT YOUR DOG YOU WERE NERVOUS/UNSURE ABOUT?

WHAT WAS YOUR DOG DOING WHEN YOU FIRST MET?

WHAT WAS IT LIKE BRINGING YOUR DOG HOME FOR THE FIRST TIME?

WHAT ARE SOME OF THE FIRST THINGS YOU AND YOUR DOG DID TOGETHER?

ADVOCACY

Dogs aren't robots! It sounds silly but, unfortunately, dogs are increasingly expected in contemporary society to act like perfect robots. Dogs are expected to be seen and not heard. They are increasingly expected to be comfortable in situations and settings that are very unnatural to them: busy city streets, dog parks, outdoor cafes, etc. While some dogs handle these situations extremely well, most can become stressed or anxious. Most of our dogs, even well-socialized, emotionally stable dogs, have things that make them nervous or uncomfortable, or that they just simply don't like. Dogs are not public property; they are not petting zoo animals walking down the street or animatronic stuffed toys. They shouldn't be forced to greet people or other dogs if they are uncomfortable or uninterested in doing so. People see dogs and get overly excited; they forget their manners and just want to pet or play with them. Some dogs are excited by strangers, while others can be various degrees less excited, from being outright uncomfortable and reactive to just being hesitant or uninterested. The same is true for dogs greeting other dogs. Would you run up to a stranger you don't know on the street and start hugging them and playing with their hair? No, of course not, but that's what people want do to our dogs every day if given the opportunity.

It can feel uncomfortable to tell people no when they ask to pet our dogs, or to ask people to interact with them in very specific ways, but we owe it to our dogs to advocate for them. They look to us for guidance and rely on us to make the world safe for them and to be their advocates. For this section, we're going to think about ways that we can help our dogs translate their needs to the world.

WHAT ARE SOME THINGS THAT MAKE YOUR DOG UNHAPPY, NERVOUS, OR UNCOMFORTABLE?

WHEN DO THESE SITUATIONS COME UP?

HOW DOES YOUR DOG REACT IN THOSE SITUATIONS?

WHAT DO YOU DO?

ARE THERE WAYS THAT YOU COULD INTERVENE BEFORE YOUR DOG GETS STRESSED, UPSET, OR NERVOUS?

_____

_____

_____

One of the hardest parts of advocating for our dogs is knowing what to say—it can help a lot to practice in advance and have a script well rehearsed.

WHAT ARE SOME THINGS YOU CAN SAY TO PEOPLE WHO WANT TO DO SOMETHING THAT WILL MAKE YOUR DOG UNCOMFORTABLE?

_____

_____

_____

Practice, practice, practice! Practice being your dog's best advocate every time you go out in public together. Our goal is for our dogs' to trust that we will handle situations and always keep them safe and comfortable.

DO YOU NOTICE ANY DIFFERENCE IN YOUR DOG'S CONFIDENCE OR BEHAVIOR AFTER YOU HAVE BEGUN DOING MORE INTENTIONAL ADVOCACY?

_____

_____

_____

GOAL SETTING

All of us want to have better relationships with our dogs, and one of the best ways to achieve that is to be intentional about the time that you have together. Dogs have a lifespan so much shorter than our own. We have an incredible opportunity to make their time with us as joyful, enriching, and safe as possible. What are some things you want to commit to doing with or for your dog? things that you want to do together? training or behavior goals that you want to work on together? These don't need to be big bucket-list-style goals; they can be smaller goals like coming directly home from work and taking your dog from a walk every day before meeting up with friends, or taking a sport class together. The best way to achieve a goal is to keep the goals realistic and to outline simple steps that you can take to achieve that goal.

GOAL SETTING

WHAT DO YOU WISH YOUR DOG DID DIFFERENTLY?

_____

_____

_____

WHAT STEPS CAN YOU TAKE TO ACHIEVE THAT GOAL?

1. _____

2. _____

3. _____

WHAT DOES YOUR DOG WISH THAT YOU DID DIFFERENTLY?

WHAT STEPS CAN YOU TAKE TO CHANGE THAT?

1.
2.
3.

WHAT IS SOMETHING YOU AND YOUR DOG CAN WORK ON TOGETHER?

WHAT STEPS CAN YOU TAKE TO ACHIEVE THIS?

1.
2.
3.

WHAT IS SOMETHING YOU AND YOUR DOG CAN WORK ON TOGETHER?

_____

_____

WHAT STEPS CAN YOU TAKE TO ACHIEVE THIS?

1. _____

2. _____

3. _____

WHAT IS SOMETHING YOU AND YOUR DOG CAN WORK ON TOGETHER?

_____

_____

_____

WHAT STEPS CAN YOU TAKE TO ACHIEVE THIS?

1. _____

2. _____

3. _____

BEST IN SHOW!

Dog shows are a way of measuring how good dogs are; the kind of "good" being measured will depend on the kind of show. In conformation shows—where the dogs are led in circles by breed around a ring; the thing most of us think of as "dog shows"—dogs are being measured not against one another but by how well that individual dog corresponds with the recognized breed standard. Essentially, the dog who is aesthetically and structurally as close to perfect as possible wins. In other kinds of competition, like obedience, agility, scent work, etc., dogs are judged by their performance: how well and how quickly they complete a course of rainbow obstacles, or how precisely they heel at attention next to their handler, how well they stay, how well they find a specific scent, and how clearly they signal that they have done so, how fast they run...you get the idea.

Something that has been made clear to me over the years, however, is that, no matter how many ribbons a dog wins, no dog is any better than any other dog. Sure, some people (and dogs—yes really there are dogs who truly love the sports they compete in) thrive on competition, on the thrill, the gamble of getting into the ring and seeing what will happen, but your dog at home napping next to you is as much of a winner as the dogs prancing around the ring on TV (the few times a year we are lucky enough to get dog show coverage). If your dog were to design a show, what would they win first place for? The first time my youngest dog went into the obedience ring, she rolled and rolled and rolled; I couldn't stop laughing, and still to this day we tell her that she won first place at rolling.

Create a dog show for your dog! You can make it as small as you like by just filling out these questions, or as elaborate as you wish. Consider making an award or ribbon for your dog, put it on the fridge, display it on social media. Is your dog the best at napping? Snacking? Playing, making you laugh? Cheering you up? No matter what your dog's talents are, celebrate them.

WHAT DOES YOUR DOG DO BEST?

WHAT DOES YOUR DOG LOVE MOST?

WHAT IS CUTEST ABOUT YOUR DOG?

IN WHAT WAYS IS YOUR DOG SMART?

IN WHAT WAYS IS YOUR DOG CLEVER

WHAT IS THE FUNNIEST THING YOUR DOG DOES?

_____

_____

_____

WHAT IS THE WEIRDEST THING YOUR DOG DOES?

_____

_____

_____

IS THERE SOMETHING YOUR DOG DOES THAT'S DIFFERENT FROM OTHER DOGS YOU KNOW?

_____

_____

_____

_____ (your dog's name) is Best in Show for _____

(Use the next page to design an award for your dog!)

LIVE THE DREAM

You don't have to wait for New Year's Eve to set resolutions for the new year, in fact, it's probably better that you don't wait. Something like over fifty percent of New Year's resolutions end up getting abandoned—yikes! There is a bumper-sticker saying, "I work hard to give my dog a better life." This rings true for a lot of us! What kind of life do you and your dog have together?

WHAT KIND OF LIFE DO YOU WANT TO HAVE WITH YOUR DOG?

WHAT DO YOU WANT TO DO MORE OF?

WHAT DO YOU WANT TO DO LESS OF?

DO YOU HAVE ANY REGRETS ABOUT WHAT YOU HAVE DONE WITH YOUR DOG?

_____

_____

IF YES, WHAT HAVE YOU DONE OR WHAT CAN YOU DO TO CHANGE THAT?

_____

_____

WHAT ARE YOUR DREAMS WITH YOUR DOG?

_____

_____

WHAT AREAS OF YOUR LIFE WITH YOUR DOG DO YOU WANT TO BE MORE INTENTIONAL
ABOUT?

_____

_____

IF YOUR DOG COULD TALK, WHAT DO YOU THINK THEY WOULD SAY ABOUT YOUR LIFE
TOGETHER?

_____

_____

IF YOU SPENT TEN, FIFTEEN, TWENTY, OR THIRTY MINUTES A DAY INTENTIONALLY FOCUSED ON YOUR DOG, WHAT WOULD YOU WANT TO SPEND THAT TIME DOING?

_____

_____

_____

GOAL SETTING

What goals do you have with your dog? These could be training goals; anything from teaching your dog a new trick to entering a dog show! Or, they could be goals focused on spending more intentional time with your dog.

SET A GOAL:

_____

_____

_____

ACTION STEP—WHAT DO YOU NEED TO DO TO MAKE THAT GOAL A REALITY?

_____

_____

_____

GROWING TOGETHER

Once you have a dog you are a different kind of person. Dogs make us better, more responsible, kinder, gentler people. Dogs inspire us to be our best selves, they give us so much, and in return we sacrifice a lot to give them the best lives possible. Mostly this is a good thing, but realistically, there can also be challenges and hard times and heartache when we share our lives with dogs and become immersed with them. Dogs change our lives in profound ways...

HOW HAS YOUR DOG CHANGED YOUR LIFE?

WHAT IS SOMETHING YOU DO NOW THAT YOU HAVE A DOG THAT YOU WOULD NEVER HAVE DONE BEFORE?

WAS IT HARD TO HAVE YOUR DOG AT FIRST—MAYBE THEY CHEWED THINGS UP OR KEPT YOU AWAKE ALL NIGHT?

HOW HAS THAT GOTTEN EASIER OVER TIME?

WHAT DO YOU WISH YOU HAD KNOWN BEFORE YOU BROUGHT YOUR DOG HOME?

WHAT ABOUT HAVING A DOG IS DIFFERENT FROM WHAT YOU THOUGHT IT WOULD BE LIKE?

WHAT ARE THE THINGS YOU THINK ABOUT NOW THAT YOU WOULDN'T HAVE BEFORE YOU GOT A DOG?

HOW HAVE YOU AS A PERSON CHANGED SINCE YOU BROUGHT YOUR DOG HOME?

YOUR DOG'S NAME—ORIGIN STORY

Names always hold significant meaning—they're who we are in the world—and the same is true for our dogs! Some dogs have popular names, and dog names goes in and out of style just like baby names. From Fido and King to Bella and Spot. How did your dog get their name? Did you pick it? Did a rescue or shelter pick a name for your dog and you decided to keep it? Did your dog come into your life with a name that you changed? Did you know right away what your dog's name would be, or did you go through a whole list to find the right name?

MY DOG'S NAME IS: _____

DID YOU NAME YOUR DOG?

_____

_____

_____

HOW DID YOUR DOG GET THEIR NAME?

_____

_____

_____

IS THERE ANY SYMBOLISM BEHIND YOUR DOG'S NAME?

_____

_____

_____

DID YOU CONSIDER OTHER NAMES FOR YOUR DOG? IF SO, WHAT WERE THEY?

TRAINING TIP

Does your dog respond to their name? You always want to make sure that, for your dog, their name means something good. Never use your dog's name in an angry or upset tone. A great way to make positive associations with your dog's name and start to train them to watch or focus on you when you use their name, is to "charge it." Take a handful of treats your dog likes, then say their name and treat, say their name and treat... Repeat this over several sessions. You aren't asking your dog to sit or do anything else, just say their name and treat. Your dog is quickly going to associate you saying their name with a reward, so they'll automatically begin looking at you anytime you use their name. This is an easy, quick game to build and reward focus!

PLAY!

Dogs love to play, but they all love to play differently. You probably have noticed that your dog has some favorite games. Many dogs like to play with toys, but not all dogs play with them in the same way, some dogs are fetch-aholics, while others prefer to play tug.

WHAT KIND OF GAMES DOES YOUR DOG LIKE TO PLAY?

_____

_____

WHAT KIND OF GAMES DOES YOUR DOG LIKES TO PLAY WITH PEOPLE?

_____

_____

WHAT KINDS OF GAMES DOES YOUR DOG LIKE TO PLAY WITH OTHER DOGS?

_____

_____

HOW OFTEN DO YOU AND YOUR DOG PLAY?

_____

_____

Try to find time every day to play with your dog. Even if it's just for a few minutes, the time you spend playing together will really positively influence your relationship.

NATURAL INSTINCT

All dogs are different, and each breed of dog was originally developed for different reasons. Some dogs were developed just for companionship, while others (both large and small) were bred to guard and to draw attention to the presence of strangers, and others still were developed to herd sheep and other livestock, or to hunt rodents, assist hunters by retrieving game, rescue people from drowning, chase down game, and so much more!

WHAT KIND OF DOG DO YOU HAVE? IF YOU HAVE A MIXED BREED DOG, WHAT BREEDS IS YOUR DOG MIXED WITH (IF YOU KNOW). IF YOU DON'T KNOW, WHAT GUESSES DO YOU HAVE?

_____

_____

_____

GO ONLINE OR TO YOUR LOCAL LIBRARY AND DO A LITTLE BIT OF RESEARCH ABOUT THE BREED(S) OF DOG YOU HAVE. WHAT WERE THEY ORIGINALLY BRED FOR?

_____

_____

_____

ONCE YOU KNOW A LITTLE BIT MORE ABOUT THE KIND OF ACTIVITIES OR WORK YOUR DOG'S ANCESTORS DID, IT CAN BE FUN TO THINK ABOUT HOW TO CHANNEL THAT INTO YOUR DOG'S LIFE. WHAT KIND OF ACTIVITIES OR GAMES CAN YOU THINK OF THAT WOULD ALLOW YOUR DOG TO DO A LITTLE MORE OF WHAT THEY WERE BRED TO DO?

_____

_____

_____

WHAT DOES YOUR DOG THINK OF THESE ACTIVITIES?

_____

_____

_____

There are also organized sports that allow dogs to channel their innate talents. Check out your local dog-training or kennel club for information about how to get involved. A few of the wide array of canine sports that exist include:

Barn Hunt—dogs "hunt" for rats (no rats are harmed) through and over bales of hay. This sport is open to all breeds of dogs.

Earth Dog—specifically for terrier breeds, in Earth Dogs, terrier breeds are able to search through artificial tunnels searching for rats (again no rats are harmed).

Herding—open to all breeds of dogs, but herding breeds certainly excel at this sport of moving sheep, ducks, or other livestock. Treibball is an urban version of this sport where dogs herd balls instead of animals!

Scent Work—all dogs love to smell, and while some breeds were developed with exceptional senses of smell, all dogs see much of their world through their nose. This sport channels that innate talent, with dogs searching for specific essential oils.

Fast CAT / Lure Coursing—Fast CAT is open to all breeds of dogs, but Lure Coursing is only open to scent hounds. Dogs chase a mechanical lure in a timed race.

Dock Diving—Fantastic for dogs whose breeds were developed to work in water, with dock diving, dogs dive off of docks into pools and compete to see which dog can jump the farthest.

HAVE YOU AND YOUR DOG EVER GIVEN ANY OF THESE SPORTS A CHANCE? WHAT DID YOU AND YOUR DOG THINK?

GROOMING GOALS

Keeping your dog well-groomed is essential for maintaining your pup's overall health, and it's also a wonderful way for you and your dog to bond. Depending on your dog's coat type, you may need to groom more frequently than once a week (some heavy-coated dogs require daily grooming, especially in shedding season) but for most dogs grooming each week will keep your dog clean and in good condition. Grooming is a good opportunity to get hands on with your dog, feeling for any lumps, bumps, or changes in your dog's skin. Keeping your dog's coat free of matting will promote healthier skin and prevent sores from developing.

Trimming your dog's nails with clippers or by grinding down with a dremel is extremely important. If you can hear your dog's nails on hard floors, they are probably too long. Because the quick of a dog's nail can grow quite long, you have to go slowly to begin to work longer nails back down to an appropriate length. Having their nails too long can make it hard for dogs to comfortably walk or maintain balance, and can lead to orthopedic issues. Many dogs are nervous or uncomfortable about having their nails trimmed, so it's important to introduce your dog slowly to the activity and to pair nail trims with high-value treats. Go slowly to support your dog staying comfortable and adjusting to the sensation.

Building a regular grooming routine is an important part of taking care of your dog. Keep notes of how far you make it through your grooming routine weekly, and if there are any things you want to remember, positive or negative, like the week you had to give your dog a bath because she rolled in something smelly at the park, or the week that she calmly offered her paw for you to trim her nails!

Month 1

Week 1		Week 2	
Grooming Activity:	Date:	Grooming Activity:	Date:
Notes:		Notes:	
Brushing:		Brushing:	
Nails:		Nails:	
Other:		Other:	
Week 3		Week 4	
Grooming Activity:	Date:	Grooming Activity:	Date:
Notes:		Notes:	
Brushing:		Brushing:	
Nails:		Nails:	
Other:		Other:	

Month 2

Week 1		Week 2	
Grooming Activity:	Date:	Grooming Activity:	Date:
Notes:		Notes:	
Brushing:		Brushing:	
Nails:		Nails:	
Other:		Other:	
Week 3		**Week 4**	
Grooming Activity:	Date:	Grooming Activity:	Date:
Notes:		Notes:	
Brushing:		Brushing:	
Nails:		Nails:	
Other:		Other:	

Month 3

Week 1		Week 2	
Grooming Activity:	Date:	Grooming Activity:	Date:
Notes:		Notes:	
Brushing:		Brushing:	
Nails:		Nails:	
Other:		Other:	
Week 3		Week 4	
Grooming Activity:	Date:	Grooming Activity:	Date:
Notes:		Notes:	
Brushing:		Brushing:	
Nails:		Nails:	
Other:		Other:	

How often you bathe your dog is going to depend on a variety of factors, including your dog's coat type, what kind of outdoor activities you pursue, and any allergies or skin conditions they have. A general rule of thumb is that most dogs should be bathed at minimum every three months, but bathing too frequently can be detrimental to your dog's coat and the natural oils on their skin. Unless your dog has been in something very dirty or stinky, you don't want to bathe your dog more frequently than every few weeks. Talk with your dog's breeder and/or your vet to determine how frequently is best for your dog's skin and coat type.

MEDICAL RECORDS

Dogs rely on us to keep them safe and healthy, which can be challenging because dogs can't actually tell us how they are feeling! Keeping copies of your dog's vet records—especially proof of vaccinations—somewhere easily accessible is important especially in the case of an emergency.

VET NAME: _____

VET PHONE: _____

VET ADDRESS: _____

NEXT APPOINTMENT? _____

DUE FOR? _____

CLOSEST EMERGENCY VET: _____

PHONE: _____

ADDRESS: _____

WHAT'S NORMAL FOR YOUR DOG? KEEPING TRACK OF YOUR DOG'S BASELINE HEALTH INFORMATION IS USEFUL:

_____

WEIGHT? _____

WHAT FOOD DO YOU FEED THEM?

_____

_____

_____

ANY KNOWN CONDITIONS?

MEDICATION/SUPPLEMENTS YOUR DOG TAKES MONTHLY?

MEDICATION/SUPPLEMENTS YOUR DOG TAKES DAILY?

FLEA/TICK PREVENTION?

WHEN SICK

Writing down the details of your dog's symptoms when they aren't feeling well can be very helpful with making sure your dog gets the best veterinary care. Bringing your written notes to your appointment can help you clearly and effectively communicate what's going on with your dog and help your vet reach the right diagnosis. It's so hard when our dogs are sick because they can't tell us exactly what's wrong, but the more information we can gather, the more it will help.

SYMPTOM TRACKER

PAIN?

_____

_____

_____

EATING?

_____

_____

_____

DRINKING?

_____

_____

_____

PEEING?

_____

_____

_____

POOPING?

_____

_____

_____

OTHER SYMPTOMS:

_____

_____

_____

If you have a medically fragile dog, a senior dog, or one who has been sick, I find it helpful to keep an active-symptom chart like this, including daily eating habits, in a notebook that you can keep updated daily or weekly. By keeping a close focus on your dog's health, you may be able to notice symptoms before they become serious.

It's also a good idea to keep physical proof of your dog's vaccinations. You can print the vaccinations out and put them in a folder or fold and staple them into this activity book.

LEARNING ABOUT DOGS

BLOOD DONOR

Did you know that, like people, when dogs are seriously injured or have major surgery, they might need to have blood transfusions? The blood that is used for these medical procedures comes from doggie blood donors! Many large emergency veterinary hospitals have dog blood donor programs where dogs can apply to be regular blood donors. Usually the programs look for large adult dogs who are healthy and comfortable in veterinary settings and whose owners are able to make a regular commitment of bringing their dogs to donate.

In addition to knowing that they are helping to save the lives of other dogs, often blood donor dogs get special toys and treats in recognition of their volunteer efforts.

Are you interested in seeing if your dog can be a blood donor? Contact your local veterinary hospitals and ask about their canine blood donor program!

PUPPALS

Do you and your dog want to find a way to give back to the community around you, but maybe you aren't up for being a therapy dog team? There are tons of amazing dogs who, for whatever reason, aren't cut out for the stressful nature of training to be therapy dogs, or maybe it's not something that you have time and capacity for. The American Kennel Club has come up with an amazing solution to this that enables dogs to give back to those in need from the comfort of their homes.

The AKC PupPals program sends letters "from" dogs to children who are in crisis, ill, or dealing with a hard time in their family. The dogs provide comfort and support, and try to bring a smile to children's faces with fun information about the dog's life. Because of the confidential nature of the program, the dog/handler teams never know what children receive their photographs and information, but you and your dog can rest assured that you are helping to bring a little bit of doggie joy to a child's life.

Participation in the program is free and you can learn more about it online at: www.akc.org/public-education.

At the time of writing, the process for registering your dog is to upload a cute photograph and answer a few questions about your dog's habits and favorite things to do. When your dog is approved for the program, you will receive an official certificate in the mail along with a bandanna for your dog proudly identifying them as a PupPal!

SEARCH AND RESCUE

Does your dog have an amazing nose? Do you and your dog have a strong desire to be outside and give back to your community? If so, your dog might be a candidate for training to become a search and rescue dog, with you as their handler.

Search and rescue dogs are (generally) civilian volunteer dog-and-handler teams that work in close collaboration with local law enforcement and first responders to dispatch and search for lost people near their homes as well as in response to natural disasters like earthquakes. Search and rescue teams also deploy after acts of terrorism. Dogs can be trained to search and find people in the aftermath of avalanches, as well as receive specialized training as cadaver dogs to recover human remains.

Not every dog (or handler) is a good fit for becoming a search and rescue team, as it is very strenuous work for dogs and people. This is a serious job. Search dogs and their handlers work in very demanding weather conditions. Technically, search and rescue dogs can be any breed or mixed breed of dog, but some breeds such as golden retrievers, Malinois, and German shepherds are amongst those that tend to excel at the work. Local search and rescue organizations near you will be able to provide more information about how to get involved, and will connect you with possible local mentors as well as training seminars, classes, and other opportunities to learn from search and rescue dog teams, and when/if you and your dog are ready, the process for becoming certified.

Resources: These national organizations can provide more training resources and support, and can also help you get connected with local groups to learn more about assessing your dog and learning more about how to get involved.

NASAR—National Association for Search and Rescue (NASAR.org)
American Rescue Dog Association (ardainc.org)
Search and Rescue Dogs of the United States (sardogsus.org)

QUIZ ABOUT DOGS—
HOW MUCH DO YOU KNOW?

1. Do dogs have fingerprints? _____

2. What is the smallest breed of dog? _____

3. How many teeth do dogs have? _____

4. Can dogs see when they are born? _____

5. Are dogs colorblind? _____

6. Can you teach an old dog new tricks? _____

7. Can dogs have webbed feet? _____

8. How many eyelids do dogs have? _____

9. Are there dogs who can't bark? _____

10. How many breeds of dog are there? _____

ANSWERS

1.   Similar to a fingerprint, dogs each have a unique "nose print!"

2.   Chihuahua.

3.   Adult dogs have forty-two teeth, puppies have twenty-eight teeth.

4.   No! Puppies don't open their eyes until they are approximately two weeks old.

5.   Contrary to common assumptions, dogs aren't actually colorblind! Dogs see black and white, but they also see shades of yellow and blue.

6.   Yes! Dogs are never too old to start learning!

7.   Not all dogs, but some dogs bred to work in the water, including Newfoundlands and Portuguese water dogs, have webbed toes to help them swim.

8.   Dogs have four eyelids, two that are the most visible and two in the inner corners of a dog's eye that are not generally visible in healthy dogs.

9.   The basenji is the only breed of dog who is technically "barkless," but don't let that fool you—basenji's are not silent!

10.   As of publication, the American Kennel Club recognizes 193 different breeds of dog!

DOG BEHAVIOR QUIZ

How much do you know about dogs and how they see and understand the world?

1. Can walking your dog improve their overall behavior?

    _____

2. Is your dog smarter than your neighbor's honor student?

    _____

3. A dog wagging their tail is friendly (Y/N): _____

4. Dogs chew on things when they are upset with us (Y/N): _____

5. What is piloerection? _____

6. Dogs get to know each other by sniffing each other's
    butts (Y/N): _____

7. Dogs yawn when they are tired (Y/N): _____

ANSWERS

1.   Yes! While walks aren't something that can fix behavior issues, dogs who do not get enough physical and mental stimulation are much more likely to display challenging behaviors.

2.   A clever bumper sticker, and not exactly accurate, but also not too far off. Dogs are as smart as some children! Generally, experts agree that dogs have comparable mental processing to a two-year-old child.

3.   Not always! Dogs wag their tail for a lot of reasons and in different ways. A highly erect tail may indicate agitation regardless if it is wagging; similarly, a very low-positioned tail, even with some wagging, may indicate that a dog is fearful or uncomfortable. You can't always read a dog just by looking at how their tail wags, as wagging might mean excitement and friendliness, but it could also be a sign of insecurity or even aggression. You want to instead look at a dog's whole demeanor and body language, not just the tail.

4.   False! Chewing is a very self-rewarding activity for dogs, and for puppies it's a very natural part of teething. Dogs experience the world in different sensory ways than we (generally) do, and one of those ways is by chewing. When dogs chew, they aren't trying to annoy us—even if it is our new pair of sneakers.

5.   It sounds risqué but this is actually a fancy term for what most of us call hackles, and describes when the hair on the back of your dog's neck and back stands up. Generally, dogs experience piloerection when they are stressed, agitated, or fearful about a situation.

6.   True! A common and very appropriate form of greeting between dogs is sniffing each other's butts. While it's not how you or I probably want to greet a stranger, it's a very appropriate way for dogs to greet one another and learn about each other.

7.   Sometimes! But that's not the only reason dogs yawn, it is also a sign that a dog is stressed.

SHAPING

Shaping is a method of teaching skills that most dogs pick up on very quickly and have a lot of fun with. It's also a fantastic way to teach really complicated skills to your dog, and it challenges us as trainers/canine educators because we have to be very thoughtful, intentional, and need to have fantastic timing in order to clearly communicate to our dogs so they understand exactly what we want.

SUPPLIES

- 🦴   Clicker—the best and easiest way to teach shaping is with a clicker (you know, those little boxes that make clicking noises that you can buy for a dollar or two at pet shops).
- 🦴   Treats—lots of very small, high-value treats.

If your dog isn't familiar with clicker training already, you will want to familiarize your dog to the clicker, what we call "charging" the clicker. Click the clicker and give your dog a treat. Repeat this several times so your dog understands the sound of the clicker means a treat is coming. Next incorporate your clicker into training with skills your dog already knows, like "sit." As soon as your dog's bottom touches the floor, click and treat!

PROCESS

The reason that we use a clicker when shaping (and with other training) is it enables us as trainers to have very precise communication with our dogs, and specifically to be able to "mark" or clearly communicate to our dog the exact thing they are doing that we want more of. So, for example, marking your dog shaking their body, sticking out their tongue, shaking their head, etc., are all very subtle physical movements that work well with shaping. With shaping, you will be rewarding and marking very small steps towards the desired end behavior, as opposed to luring your dog to do something, and it requires a lot of patience on your part. Most of us are so used to telling our dogs what to do, in this instance we have to really wait, listen, and trust our dog.

The more shaping training you do with your dog, the better at the game both of you will get. You can add some structure to the training session verbally if you want, I use "lets learn," but for most dogs the treats and clicker coming out is a very clear signal that some fun learning is about to take place, and your dog will be eager to start offering behaviors and puzzling out what you want.

REFLECT ON THE PROCESS OF SHAPING: HOW DID IT FEEL FOR YOU?

_____

_____

_____

HOW DO YOU PERCEIVE THE PROCESS WAS FOR YOUR DOG? DID THEY STAY ENGAGED? DID THEY SEEM FRUSTRATED?

_____

_____

_____

Shaping is only one way of learning, and while it's a lot of fun for many dogs and people, it doesn't work for everyone, and that's ok! If you or your dog find yourselves getting frustrated by the activity, don't push it—there are lots of ways to learn, and you can always revisit shaping later or leave it behind all together.

Are you feeling hooked? Clicker Expo is a fantastic annual conference that happens each year (one on the west coast and one on the east coast of the United States). You can learn more online at www.ClickerExpo.com.

CRAFTS!

DOODLE DOODLES!

Dog-watching is every dog person's favorite hobby. Use this page to draw all the dogs you see on your walk or going about your week. You don't have to be a "great artist" to draw the dogs you encounter. One of the most wonderful things about dogs is the way that they live authentically and enthusiastically in the moment—they aren't worried about being perfect, they are just having fun! Try to channel that same carefree playfulness into your doodles!

PAW-PRINT FLOWERS

These paw-print flowers make a perfect spring craft for you and your dog!

Supplies needed: nontoxic washable paint in whatever colors you like; nontoxic and washable markers; paper. You can do some painting right here on the page of this book, but you might want more paintings, so to be prepared with extra paper. You'll also want a wet washcloth to wipe off your dog's paw after the painting.

Paw painting can be messy, so this is a great activity to do outside if you have a yard or patio, or you can lay out some old newspapers, a tablecloth, or a sheet as a backdrop to protect your floor from the paint.

INSTRUCTIONS

1. Put some of the nontoxic paint onto a paper plate and gently dip your dog's paw into the paint.

2. Place your dog's paw onto the page and carefully lift up.

3. Wipe your dog's paw with the washcloth.

4. When the paint has dried, go back with your markers and doodle the stem and leaves onto the paw-prints to make flowers!

BRAIDED TUG TOYS!

Tug is a favorite game of many dogs and is a great way to bond and connect with your dog. Tugging can also be a useful game! Playing tug is a great way to redirect dogs who tend to be overly excited when playing and greeting. It's also a game that can be used to teach and reinforce self-control for your dog. Asking your dog to wait to be released to tug, signaling your dog to drop the tug toy on cue, and then highly rewarding them by releasing them back to tug, are all wonderful training opportunities. Tug is also a great way to build engagement with a shy dog or dog who lacks confidence.

Tug toys can get expensive, but you can create custom toys for your dog—no sewing required! Most fabric stores have bolts and bolts of fleece fabrics in every color and pattern imaginable. Pick a few colors or patterns that you like to create a tug toy your dog will love! You can even create themed toys to match your favorite sporting team, or make festive holiday tugs.

INSTRUCTIONS

1. Cut the fleece into three strips, each four to five inches wide and a yard long.
2. Tie the strips of fleece into a knot on one end.
3. Braid the three strips of fleece tightly together.
4. Tie a knot on the other end.
5. Playtime for your dog!

DONATION OPPORTUNITY

Does your dog already have enough toys? Make tug toys to donate to dogs who are less fortunate. These braided tug toys are perfect to donate to rescue groups and shelters as enrichment toys for dogs who are waiting for their forever families.

NO-SEW DOG BEDS

Is your dog looking for a new cozy place to nap? These no-sew beds are quick and easy to craft and make the perfect nap spot for your dog (or you can make them to donate).

SUPPLIES

- Two pieces of fleece, each one square yard (for an extra fun design, use two different fleece patterns, one for each side).
- Batting/stuffing to put inside the bed.

INSTRUCTIONS

1. To make the bed, we will start with the two fleece squares, each a yard in size. With each yard of fabric, we are going to cut strips around the perimeter of the fleece. The size of the strips is up to you: one or two inches wide is generally a good size, and approximately four inches long.

2. Cut your strips around the perimeter of both pieces of fleece. Lay the "back" side of the fleeces facing each other so the outside of the pieces are both facing outwards.

3. Tie together all of the strips, double knotting, then leave half of one side of the rectangle open to leave room to get the stuffing in.

4. Add stuffing, as much as you want. Remember that as your dog lies on the bed, the stuffing will break down, so it's a good idea to start with some extra stuffing.

5. Finish double knotting the remaining strips to finish closing up the bed.

6.   Fluff it up to make sure the stuffing is evenly distributed and give it to your dog!

EXTRAS

Get seasonal fabric and make festive holiday beds for your dog! Store the beds with your other holiday decorations and trade them out for each season!

For a fun idea, you can get a group of friends together with a lot of fleece and make a large batch of these no-sew beds to donate to a shelter or rescue group near you. This is something you could do for the winter holiday season, or any time of year.

> **Note:** Contact rescue groups and shelters ahead of time to make sure that these kinds of donations will be useful at this time.

SNUFFLE MAT!
DIY BRAIN EXERCISER FOR YOUR DOG!

Dogs experience the world through their nose! A dog's sense of smell is not only their strongest sense, sniffing is also extremely enriching for our dogs. In addition, sniffing can be very stress relieving for dogs who are stressed, and a fantastic way for them to relax and decompress during or after stressful experiences. Using a snuffle mat allows a dog to eat slower (if you are using the mat as a way to feed them some or all of their meals), which can aid with digestion and provides an enriching, positive outlet for dogs to be able to use their nose.

One self-directed, scent-based game your dog can play is puzzling out a snuffle mat. Snuffle mats can be commercially purchased or you can make one on your own for your dog! Snuffle mats give dogs an outlet for their desire to sniff, are highly rewarding, and are a great way to occupy your dog inside during cold or wet weather or to entertain a dog who needs to be kept a little quieter while recovering from surgery or other medical procedures (always be sure to check with your vet if this level of activity is ok).

SUPPLIES

- Two to three yards of fleece—you can buy whatever is cheap and on sale or you can pick a color scheme that matches your decor. I'm a big believer in the idea that dog toys and gear don't have to be ugly! You can combine multiple colors, textures, and widths of fleece to add additional texture to your matt.
- A rubber matt with holes in it—these are commonly sold as "anti-fatigue" mats, made for standing on in industrial kitchens. These can be found relatively inexpensively online or at big-box retailers and hardware stores. Depending on the size

of your dog, you can also use plastic craft mesh as your base, though this works better for smaller dogs. For most dogs, a mat that is twelve square inches is a great size.

INSTRUCTIONS

1. Cut the fleece into strips one to three inches wide by six to eleven inches in length.

2. Double knot your fleece strips through each hole, going all the way down the length of the mat row by row.

3. Go back and double knot the fleece strips (it helps to use a different color so you can see easier where you are going) through the holes on the diagonal making an "x" shape with your fleece.

4. Once you have tied fleece through the whole mat, you will have one side that is flat (that's the bottom) and the other side that has the knots and the ends of all the fleece strips—this is the side that will be fun for your dog!

5. Take some dry kibble (it's a great way to make mealtime more exciting for your dog) and/or some dry treats that your dog likes—you want to avoid anything wet or moist as it will make the mat messy—and sprinkle them through the mat. Show your dog the snuffle mat and encourage them to start searching—most dogs don't need to be asked twice!

Note: Be sure to supervise your dog while they are playing with the snuffle mat—most dogs are happy just to sniff, but of course it could be a safety hazard for any dog that did chew off pieces of the fleece or mat trying to get at the treats.

DINNER IS SERVED!

Is your dog bored at mealtime? Design a custom placemat for your dog! If your dog is a heavy chewer, like with any other placemat, it's a good idea to make sure to supervise your dog while eating on the placemat to make sure they don't decide to chew on it!

SUPPLIES

- Art supplies of your choosing: markers, colored pencils, paint, glitter, etc.
- Legal-size pieces of white (or other colored) paper. When your placemat is done, you'll be taking it to your local printing or office-supply store in order to laminate the placemats.

Some ideas: Write your dog's name, place arrows for where the food and/or water bowls should go, doodle your dog's favorite things: toys, outings, friends, places, or make it look like a fancy restaurant menu! You can even make these placemats for different seasons and holidays and trade them out! Remember you can even decorate both sides and flip it over to give your dog two placemats in one!

USE THE NEXT PAGE TO DOODLE DIFFERENT DESIGN IDEAS FOR YOUR DOG'S PLACEMAT. USE YOUR IMAGINATION!

When you find an idea you like, get your paper and start to recreate the design on the actual placemat, laminate, and use!

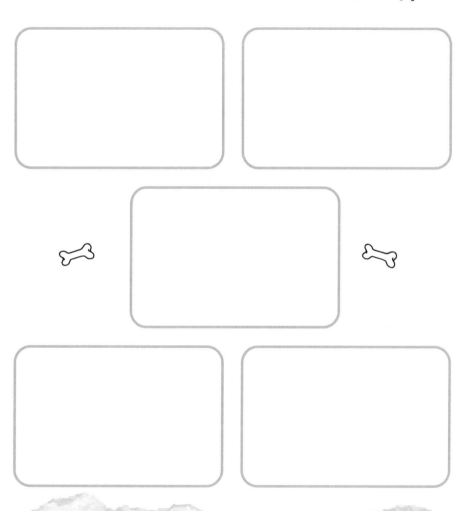

CANINE MASTERPIECE!

For this activity, your dog is going to take control of the page and let out their inner artist by actually drawing or painting in this book!

SUPPLIES

- 🐾 Washable and nontoxic markers or paints
- 🐾 A paintbrush
- 🐾 Toilet paper tube
- 🐾 Treats

INSTRUCTIONS

You can teach your dog to just hold the marker or paintbrush, but I find it easier to use a handle which gives the dog a better grip and makes it easier for your dog to get the hang of drawing. You can make a handle in different ways: I use a toilet-paper tube because it's cheap and easy, but you could also use a dowel or a piece of PVC if you would like something more durable. If you are using a toilet-paper tube, poke a hole in one side with a pencil and push the back end of the marker into the hole so that the tip is facing out.

1. If your dog already knows hold, ask your dog to hold the marker attachment and then give it back to you, praise/click, and treat. If your dog doesn't yet know hold, start with a toy your dog is already comfortable having in their mouth. Hold the toy out to your dog click, treat, and praise as your dog sniffs the toy. After a few repetitions you can start to slowly up your criteria, waiting until your dog mouths the toy before click/treat/reward. Very slowly start to build up duration, fractions of a second at a time,

and start to introduce your verbal cues like "hold." (See page 212 for more tips on teaching "hold.")

2. When your dog is comfortably able to hold the pen, ask your dog to nose target this page of the book. Praise/click/treat when your dog touches the page.

3. Next, ask your dog to hold the marker and ask for your dog to target the book. As the marker touches the book praise/click/treat! You can add in verbal cues for this trick: "draw" or "art" are good options.

Don't forget to trade out the marker for different colors. Feel free to rotate this page of the book so that your dog has more room to "draw" and create more elaborate designs!

FLUFF ART!

KNITTING

Is your dog a big shedder? All that fluff you brush off can actually be useful for crafting. Dog-fur inspired crafts are nothing new.

Fur that has been brushed off of your dog (not fur that has been cut off) can be spun into yarn the same way that sheep or alpaca wool is! You can get old fashioned and learn how to card and spin the fluff into yarn yourself, or there are companies that you can send the clean dog fur to and they will return it to you as yarn that you can then craft with. The yarn can be turned into anything from scarves and hats to a special keepsake blanket!

DONATE TO WILDLIFE!

If you aren't feeling especially crafty, you can take your dog's fur after grooming and put it outside in your yard or in a local park! Birds will pick up the fluff and use it to make nests!

ORNAMENTS

Most craft stores have clear plastic (they also have glass but I prefer plastic) Christmas bulb-shaped ornaments. The tops of these ornaments are removable, and while most artists put paint inside, you can give this craft a doggie twist by packing the inside with clean dog hair! This can serve as a special holiday keepsake each year on your tree. You can also use paint pens to decorate the outside of the bulb with your dog's name or doodles of your dog and the things you do together!

PHOTO PROPS!

Taking photos of or with your dog is a great way to capture special moments together, but your pictures don't have to be serious! Make some silly photo props and have an impromptu photo shoot with your dog. Exaggerated designs like huge cartoon dog bones can be fun, as well as silly props like beards, moustaches, monocles, sunglasses, top hats, or giant bows! There's no limit to the funny props you can create! You can also make signs with funny sayings or phrases like "I didn't do it," that you can hold up with your dog.

SUPPLIES

- Dowels, skewers, or chopsticks
- Tape
- Construction paper or cardstock
- Markers, paint, and/or colored pencils—something that you can outline or color your props with
- Scissors

INSTRUCTIONS

1. On the construction paper or cardstock (cardstock will work best), sketch or trace the outline of different shapes.

2. Cut out each of the photo props that you draw.

3. Add any colors or details you want.

4. Attach a dowel, skewers, or chopsticks to the prop with tape.

Next, you'll want to show the props to your dog. Have cookies ready and treat your dog for being near the props. If your dog isn't concerned about being near to the props, slowly hold them up to your dog and treat. If your dog acts fearful or concerned at any point, back up and start rewarding them for just being near the props. Once your dog is comfortable with the props being held near him, you're ready for your photo shoot!

IN THE SPACE BELOW, DOODLE IDEAS YOU HAVE FOR PROPS OR PASTE IN PHOTOS YOU TOOK!

SILHOUETTE ART

Want to give your crafts a personalized canine touch? Silhouettes can jazz up any craft project and give your work a classic cameo-like touch. For this to work, you'll want to take a photograph of your dog standing in profile with their head facing forward. Print out the picture—you can use a home or work printer (shh, don't tell your boss) for this because you don't need it to be high quality.

INSTRUCTIONS

1. Take your photo of your dog and a blank piece of paper. You can use tracing paper if you have it, or just plain computer paper or notebook paper. If you are using computer paper or notebook paper in order to do your trace, you'll want to hold the picture and paper up to your computer screen or to a window to create a DIY light box and make it easier to trace.

2. Once you have an outline of your dog's silhouette you'll want to cut it out so that you can use it as a stencil (if you want to repeatedly use the stencil, you can trace your silhouette onto a piece of cardstock which will last longer, though it will be harder to use on rounded objects). Now you're ready to go!

3. Place your dog's silhouette onto the object you're looking to draw it onto, like a pumpkin or a vase, or even a decorative piece of wood or plate. Trace around your dog's silhouette using a pencil or marker depending on the surface you are crafting onto.

4. Carve out the silhouette if you're working on a pumpkin, or take paints, markers, or other craft supplies and color in your dog. You can aim for realistic designs or be creative. Doodle your dog's favorite things into their silhouette, add stars, sprinkle glitter—let your creativity take over!

STUFFED FROZEN TREATS

Stuffing "Kong's" or other hollow, hard-rubber toys and then freezing them is a great option if you are looking for a way to keep your dog entertained for long periods of time. By freezing the treats inside the toy, it will slow down how quickly your dog is able to eat the treats, and keep them occupied for longer.

Some stuffers most dogs enjoy include:

- Squeeze Cheese
- Canned pumpkin
- Peanut butter
- Treats
- Commercial "Kong Stuffers" spray and creams
- Chews
- Dry kibble
- Soaked kibbles

What combinations can you come up with for your dog? Write them below and record what your dog thinks!

STUFFED RECIPES:

MY DOG'S REACTION:

STUFFED RECIPES:

MY DOG'S REACTION:

STUFFED RECIPES:

MY DOG'S REACTION:

STUFFED RECIPES:

_____

_____

MY DOG'S REACTION:

_____

_____

STUFFED RECIPES:

_____

_____

MY DOG'S REACTION:

_____

_____

STUFFED RECIPES:

_____

_____

MY DOG'S REACTION:

_____

_____

CHASE BUBBLES

Bubbles are a fun, cheap, and easy way to keep your dog active. You can purchase dog specific bubbles, including some that are flavored like bacon and peanut butter. But you can also use nontoxic/kid-safe bubbles, just be sure to read the ingredients to ensure there is nothing toxic to dogs in them.

Chasing bubbles is a lot of fun for dogs. You can play this game inside, though it can get a bit messy, so you probably want to play this outside. Get your dog's attention and blow a few bubbles: how does your dog react?

_____

_____

_____

_____

BLOW SOME ONTO THE PAGE AND TRACE THE OUTLINE OF THE BUBBLE.

SEASONAL ACTIVITIES!

DOG HOLIDAYS

Get your calendar out and start thinking about all the fun ways that you can incorporate dog-themed holidays into your year! This is a roundup of all the dog-centered holidays I could find! I hope that you and your dog have fun observing, researching, volunteering, or just celebrating the amazingness of dogs!

Don't see a holiday that speaks to you and your dog? You can also make up your own and try to get your dog's friends to start celebrating!

WHEN IS YOUR DOG'S BIRTHDAY? _____

IF YOU AND YOUR DOG WERE TO MAKE UP A HOLIDAY, WHAT WOULD IT BE?

_____

WHEN WOULD IT BE? _____

CANINE HOLIDAYS

JANUARY

National Train Your Dog Month

Unchain a Dog Month—Volunteer to help spread awareness about how important it is!

January 29—National Seeing-Eye Dog Day

FEBRUARY

Dog Dental Health Month

Spay/Neuter Awareness Month

Pet Theft Awareness Day

MARCH

Poison Prevention Month

March 20—International Day of Happiness

March 23—National Puppy Day

March 30—Take a Walk in the Park Day

APRIL

National Heartworm Awareness Month

National Pet First Aid Awareness Month

Lyme Disease Awareness/ Prevention Month

First Wednesday in April—National Walking Day

April 11—National Dog Therapy Appreciation Day

April 23—Lost Dog Awareness Day

Last Sunday in April—Pet Parents Appreciation Day

MAY

Chip Your Dog Month

May 1—National Purebred Dog Day

May 3—National Specially-abled Dog Day

JUNE

National Pet Preparedness Month

First Friday following Father's Day—Take Your Dog to Work Day (see page 17)

JULY

National Dog Loss Prevention Month

July 15—National Pet Fire Safety Day

July 31—National Mutt Day

AUGUST

Immunization Awareness Month

August 10—National Spoil Your Dog Day

August 26—National Dog Day!

SEPTEMBER

National Service Dog Month

Natural Disaster Preparedness Month

Third Saturday in September—National Puppy Mill Awareness Day

September 28—World Rabies Day

OCTOBER

National Adopt a Shelter Dog Month

National Animal Safety and Protection Month

October 4—World Animal Day

Third week of October—National Veterinary Technician Week

NOVEMBER

National Pet Cancer Awareness Month

Senior Pet Month/ National Adopt a Senior Pet Month

First week of November—Animal Shelter Appreciation Week

November 1—National Cook for Your Dog Day

November 13—World Kindness Day

DECEMBER

December 2—National Mutt Day (yes, there are two of these, mutts are just that great!)

December 5—International Volunteer Day

FROZEN TREASURE HUNT

This is a fun summer activity, but it can be messy so better enjoyed outside. Take a large silicone baking pan or bowl and gather a variety of toys that your dog likes. For this activity you will want to pick toys that will be ok in water, like solid rubber toys, tennis balls, etc., as well as treats your dog likes. Put the toys and treats into the silicone baking pan, fill it with water, and put in the freezer. When the bowl is completely frozen, flip it upside down onto a cookie sheet and remove the silicone bowl. Then bring your dog outside and allow her to explore the ice and all the treasures hidden within. It should keep her busy for a little while!

WHAT DID YOU PUT IN THE ICE?

_____

_____

_____

WHAT DID YOUR DOG THINK?

_____

_____

_____

BIRTHDAY PARTY

Your dog is your best friend, so it's only natural that you want to throw them a birthday party! Some of us know the day that our dogs were born, and some of us have no idea because our dogs were rescued. The great thing about our furry friends is that, if you're ready to party, they are all in, so you can pick any day and claim it as your dog's birthday. Many of us, if we don't know exactly what day our dog was born, will either pick a date close to when they likely were born, or we'll celebrate the day that our dog came home, their "gotcha" day, as our dog's birthday.

WHAT DAY DO YOU CELEBRATE YOUR DOG'S BIRTHDAY?

_____

MAKE A LIST OF YOUR DOG'S FAVORITE THINGS:

_____   _____

_____   _____

_____   _____

_____   _____

_____   _____

Read back over your list and circle any of the things that your dog loves that you might be able to incorporate into their birthday.

INVITATIONS

Consider who you want to invite: if your dog is quiet and not very social, you can skip this step, but if there are people and/or other dogs your dog enjoys spending time with, consider inviting them to a birthday party for your dog! Make or purchase invitations. You can just send a text message, but actually making an invitation adds to the fun of the event. Dollar stores often have kid's birthday-party-invitation packs for under a dollar, so this is something you can do cheaply.

MAKE A LIST OF YOUR DOG'S FAVORITE PEOPLE AND/OR OTHER DOGS:

_____   _____

_____   _____

_____   _____

_____   _____

_____   _____

_____   _____

LOCATION

Pick a location for the party. If you have space at your home for the party, that is probably the easiest, but many dog daycares, training facilities, dog pools, and other dog businesses are happy to rent out their spaces for birthday parties and other gatherings for dogs. You could also plan to meet up with everyone at a favorite park. Make sure the location you pick is one that your dog will enjoy!

BRAINSTORM LOCATION IDEAS:

_____   _____

_____   _____

_____   _____

_____   _____

_____   _____

_____   _____

MENU

There are many commercially available dog's birthdays cakes and cupcakes available, and an increasing number of doggie bakeries are springing up in local communities who will be happy to bake the birthday cake of your dog's dreams, or you could get creative and craft your own cake! Don't forget to have some snacks available for people, and plenty of fresh water for the dogs (and people).

SNACK OPTIONS:

_____   _____

_____   _____

_____   _____

_____   _____

_____   _____

_____   _____

GAMES

Party games aren't just for kids! Be sure to have party games planned for your dog's birthday. Some favorites are bobbing for tennis balls—if you have a baby pool, fill the pool with water and drop in as many tennis balls as you like. Let the dogs in one at a time (don't let multiple dogs go at the same time as it can cause issues between the dogs), set a timer for one minute, and see how many balls each dog can retrieve out of the water!

Looking for a less messy game? Have a trick contest, staying contest (who can stay the longest), or a talent show!

PRESENTS

Don't forget to spoil your dog with their favorite treats and toys on their birthday, but most important is spending time with your dog!

INSERT A PICTURE OF YOUR DOG'S BIRTHDAY PARTY CELEBRATION HERE!

GARDENING

As spring approaches, an exciting way to enjoy the season is to do some gardening with your dog! If you have a yard, you can plan an entire garden together, but if you live in an apartment you can also put small plants in your windows or on your balcony.

Find a dog-friendly nursery or hardware store. In most areas, garden centers tend to be dog friendly, but it's always a good idea to call in advance and make it an outing with your dog by bringing them with you to pick out your plants.

Select plants that are safe for dogs in case your dog decides to give the plant a little nibble. If you aren't certain about the safety of a particular plant, it's a good idea to double check before purchasing it. The ASPCA poison control center is a good resource for double checking the safety of plants. You can pick decorative plants, or for some added fun, you can pick edible plants that you and your dog can grow and tend together, and then, when they are ripe you can share in the spoils of garden!

Green beans, carrots, blueberries, pumpkins, sweet potatoes, spinach, broccoli, watermelons, and peas are a few fruits and vegetables that are generally safe for dogs.

WHERE DID YOU AND YOUR DOG GO TO BUY PLANTS?

WHAT DID YOUR DOG THINK OF THE NURSERY?

_____

_____

_____

WHAT PLANTS DID YOU AND YOUR DOG SELECT?

_____

_____

_____

_____

KEEP TRACK OF HOW YOUR GARDEN GROWS, AND IF YOU BOUGHT EDIBLE PLANTS,
REPORT BACK ON WHAT YOUR DOG THOUGHT OF WHAT YOU GREW!

_____

_____

_____

_____

_____

MAKE HALLOWEEN GOODIE BAGS FOR DOGS IN YOUR NEIGHBORHOOD

Trick or treat! This Halloween, don't just prepare candy for the kids in your neighborhood, have goodie bags ready for any canine trick-or-treaters. For safety, I would advise purchasing sealed, sample-size dog treats instead of packing up treats yourself. Don't want to give treats? Collect dog toys of various sizes in clearance sections of pet stores over the year and have them ready in a bucket for Halloween.

If your neighborhood has a local social-media group or email list, you can post that you'll have doggie trick-or-treat goodies (the same way that people often do if they have allergy friendly treats for kids) to make sure you get more canine trick-or-treaters.

KEEP A LIST OF ALL THE DOGS YOU GET AS TRICK-OR-TREATERS AT YOUR DOOR AND WHAT THEIR COSTUMES ARE!

Safety Note: Halloween can be a very scary holiday for dogs. Make sure that your dog is safely secured away from the door or leashed to you (if very social) to make sure they don't get spooked by the masks and costumes which can spook even the most stable dogs.

DOG HALLOWEEN COSTUMES

Getting dressed up for Halloween is a lot of fun for us, but it can be stressful for our dogs. The good news: it doesn't have to be, and can actually be as fun for our dogs as it is for us! The key to a successful dressed-up Halloween with your dog is planning ahead. If you pick a costume for your dog the day of Halloween and just throw the costume on, unless your dog is very experienced wearing costumes, it's probably not going to be a very fun or successful evening for them. Instead, come up with costume ideas well in advance so you can prepare your dog for the costume. Costumes are a big part of the holiday for a lot of people, and not only can you make fun outfits for your dog, there are also many pre-made ones available. Unfortunately, while a lot of these costumes are cute, they aren't necessarily designed with a dog's comfort in mind.

COSTUME ADVICE

- Find or make a costume that your dog can fit comfortably in and which is not restrictive for their limbs.
- Be wary of outfits with hats or headpieces. Some dogs are fine with these, but many find them uncomfortable and stressful.
- Plan your dog's costume as far in advance as possible so that you have time to make sure they are comfortable for your dog, and give them time to adjust.
- Pair wearing the costume for very short sessions with lots of treats.

By slowly introducing your dog to the costume and making positive associations, your dog will become comfortable wearing any costume and will be happy wearing it not only for a quick picture but for a whole evening of festivities.

BRAINSTORM HALLOWEEN COSTUME IDEAS FOR YOUR DOG:

WHAT COSTUME DID YOU PICK FOR YOUR DOG?

Once you decide on a theme for your dog's Halloween costume, the next step is to find or make a costume. Most dogs struggle with hats or head props—though some dogs can become comfortable with them. The key, though, when selecting a Halloween costume for your dog, is to find one that fits well and isn't restrictive. We want our dogs to be cute but not wrapped up like mummies and uncomfortable! Make sure your dog has full range of motion in the costume you select, and that it isn't so baggy as to constitute any kind of tripping hazard for your dog.

Get your dog's costume as early as possible and slowly introduce your dog to the different pieces, pairing it with treats so that your dog associates the costume with good things. As your dog becomes more comfortable with the costume on, start to add in play and games while wearing the costume. This will better prepare your dog for Halloween and help them to forget they are even wearing a costume.

DOGGO HALLOWEEN PARTY!

Consider throwing a Halloween party for your dog and their closest friends, as a benefit for your favorite rescue, or as part of the festivities for your local breed group! Fun party events include a costume contest: you can have different categories in addition to "best costume," including "best group," "best use of props," etc.

For activities, you can take a costumed walk, have a trick competition, or bob for hotdogs! For this activity, be sure that dogs only play one at a time to avoid any kind of conflict between them over food. Put bits of hotdog in a baby pool and see how many each dog can collect in a short period of time. The dog who eats the most hotdog pieces is the winner!

You can also do pumpkin painting—get (real or decorative) small pumpkins and have each of the guests paint their dog or a spooky version of their dog onto the pumpkins!

Did you have a Halloween party with your dog? Share about the experience here and paste in a picture from the party and/or of your dog in their costume!

WHO DID YOU INVITE?

_____   _____   _____

_____   _____   _____

_____   _____   _____

_____   _____   _____

_____   _____   _____

WHAT ACTIVITIES DID YOU DO?

DOG EASTER-EGG HUNT

Is your dog good at searching? This Easter, throw your dog their very own Easter-egg hunt! For this activity, you will want to get an assortment of plastic eggs. Be sure to supervise your dog when searching for eggs, as the plastic eggs can easily shatter if your dog chews on them, and could become a choking hazard.

Get small treats, the smellier the better, and fill the plastic eggs with one treat in each egg. Next, while your dog is in another room, hide the plastic eggs in places that your dog can reach. Keep track below where you hid your eggs so that you can make sure to get them all.

Keep one egg aside to show your dog.

WHERE DID YOU HIDE EGGS?	WHICH EGGS DID YOUR DOG FIND FIRST?

ADVENT CALENDAR

Most of us don't need any help remembering that Christmas is on the way, but advent calendars are a fun way to ring in the season and give ourselves a small treat every day of December as we wait for the big day. Once upon a time, advent calendars were only for children, but now—with treats from socks to booze—there are plenty of advent calendars made with adults in mind. Most of us involve our dogs in holiday festivities, from stockings to gifts to holiday meals—so what else do our dogs need? Advent calendars! I'm a bit embarrassed about how long it took me to start including my dogs in this tradition, but now that I have, there is no going back; they love it, and I love watching them get so happy!

At any craft store, you should be able to purchase a plain and empty advent calendar in various shapes and sizes, from simple boxes to Christmas-tree shapes. If you don't want to purchase an advent-calendar setup, you can inexpensively purchase or collect twenty-four small boxes that you can fill with special treats (or depending on the size of your boxes and the size of toys that are safe for your dog, toys).

BELOW MAKE A LIST OF THE KINDS OF TREATS YOU WANT TO COLLECT TO FILL YOUR
DOG'S ADVENT CALENDAR WITH:

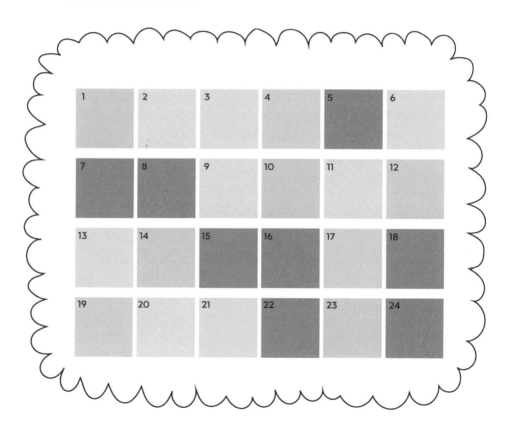

WHAT DID YOUR DOG THINK OF OPENING THEIR ADVENT CALENDAR EACH DAY? DID YOUR DOG START TO ANTICIPATE THE DAILY RITUAL OF OPENING A BOX?

WHAT OTHER CHRISTMAS FESTIVITIES DO YOU AND YOUR DOG ENJOY? WHAT NEW ONES DO YOU WANT TO START?

DO YOU TAKE YOUR DOG FOR PICTURES WITH SANTA? HOW DID IT GO?

SANDBOX

Does your dog love the beach? You can bring the magic of digging in the sand into your home by creating a summertime dig box for your dog! This activity can be a bit messy, so you'll want to keep it outside or in an easily cleaned area of your home, like a deck or balcony. Unfortunately, a dig box can also attract some attention from neighborhood cats, so it's a good idea to keep your dig box covered.

For a temporary sandbox, you can use any large and sturdy box. If you are technically inclined, you can also build a sandbox out of wood. An easy and inexpensive but sturdier option is a hard-plastic children's pool. These are usually inexpensive during the summer, and even available on clearance in the fall. Any hardware store should be able to sell you clean sand.

Fill the pool or box to the desired level, remember that your dog might be an exuberant digger, so you'll want to avoid filling the sandbox too high or you'll end up with a lot of sand outside of the box!

Add toys to the sandbox, can your dog find the buried treasure?

TAKE YOUR DOG TO WORK DAY!

First created by the group Pet Sitters International in 1999, "Take Your Dog to Work Day" is a real holiday! The event takes place annually, on the first Friday following Father's Day, and was developed as an opportunity for companies and employees to share in the joys of dogs in the workplace! Increasingly over the years, many companies have already become dog friendly on a day-to-day basis, with some companies adding benefits like pet insurance and dog parks for their employees and their dogs!

If you are interested in bringing your dog to work, talk with your HR department and discuss the possibility of your workplace participating. If you can't bring your dog to work for the day, see if it's possible for you to work from home so you can share the workday with your dog!

Note: Before bringing your dog to work, be honest about your dog's temperament and what your workplace is like. Consider if going to work will be fun for your dog or if it would be stressful: if the latter, it's a good idea to let your dog sit this activity out.

WHAT DID YOUR WORKPLACE SAY ABOUT "TAKE YOUR DOG TO WORK DAY"?

_____

_____

WERE YOU AND YOUR DOG ABLE TO PARTICIPATE?

_____

_____

IF YOU PARTICIPATED, WHAT WAS THE EXPERIENCE LIKE FOR YOU?

WHAT WAS THE RESPONSE FROM YOUR COWORKERS?

DID OTHER DOGS COME TO WORK FOR THE DAY? IF SO WHO?

WHAT DID YOUR DOG THINK OF COMING TO WORK WITH YOU?

DID YOU AND YOUR DOG DO ANYTHING SPECIAL AT WORK?

GRATITUDE

This is the kind of activity that a lot of people do around Thanksgiving, but I like to center gratitude year round. For many, dogs are the highlight of our lives; they make our days meaningful and a whole lot more fun! Having dogs can also be challenging and stressful, and it's important to reflect on the special moments you share together, everything from big adventures to cozy moments at home together!

WRITE ONE THING EVERY WEEK THIS YEAR THAT YOU ARE THANKFUL FOR ABOUT YOUR DOG AND ABOUT YOUR RELATIONSHIP:

1. _____	11. _____	21. _____
2. _____	12. _____	22. _____
3. _____	13. _____	23. _____
4. _____	14. _____	24. _____
5. _____	15. _____	25. _____
6. _____	16. _____	26. _____
7. _____	17. _____	27. _____
8. _____	18. _____	28. _____
9. _____	19. _____	29. _____
10. _____	20. _____	30. _____

31. _____   40. _____   49. _____

32. _____   41. _____   50. _____

33. _____   42. _____   51. _____

34. _____   43. _____   52. _____

35. _____   44. _____

36. _____   45. _____

37. _____   46. _____

38. _____   47. _____

39. _____   48. _____

LOOKING BACK AT YOUR YEAR TOGETHER, WHAT ARE YOUR FAVORITE MEMORIES?
FEEL FREE TO PASTE IN SOME MEMENTOES.

_____

_____

_____

_____

_____

_____

_____

EXPLORE
THE WORLD

DOG'S-CHOICE WALK

We control a lot about our dog's life, from when they eat to when they go out. Generally, the decisions we make for our dog helps them to be safe, but sometimes it can be fun to give your dog the opportunity to make decisions! Pick a day when you aren't in a rush, leash your dog, and see where they goes! A lot of times, when we walk our dogs, it is purposeful; we're walking to a destination or hurrying to finish the walk before heading off to work. For this walk, let your dog pick the pace and direction of your walk.

RECORD ALL THE PLACES YOUR DOG LED YOU—WHERE THEY CHOSE TO GO AND WHAT THEY CHOSE TO DO MIGHT SURPRISE YOU!

_____   _____

_____   _____

_____   _____

_____   _____

_____   _____

_____   _____

_____   _____

_____   _____

_____   _____

_____   _____

WALK-A-DAY CHALLENGE!

Keeping active is not only good for your dog, it's good for you too! There have been a variety of studies that show that dog guardians are healthier and happier because of their dogs! A great way to spend time with your dog is to simply take a walk together! Put your phone in your pocket, grab your dog's leash and high-value good treats to reward good behavior, and head out on a walk to explore your neighborhood!

TAKE THE THIRTY-DAY WALK CHALLENGE! COLOR IN A SQUARE EVERY DAY YOU WALK!

1	2	3	4	5	6	7	8	9	10
11	12	13	14	15	16	17	18	19	20
21	22	23	24	25	26	27	28	29	30

Are you and your dog active walkers? Consider taking the AKC's Fit Dog Challenge. It's open to any dog, purebred or mixed breed. Dogs who complete the challenge receive a complimentary award magnet for recording daily walks over a three-month period! I run a fit dog club via my YouTube channel, *Introvert Circus*. Visit the AKC's website (www.akc.org) for more information about getting your dog involved.

BOAT RIDES

Let's set sail with Fido! There are a variety of opportunities to get your dog out on the water if it's something that you think they would enjoy. For no particular reason, I really had a strong desire to bring my retired service dog, Mercury, on a boat ride, so I set out to do some research. It turns out that the paddle-boat rental outlet in Brooklyn's Prospect Park didn't actually have a dog policy—it was up to the staff working on any given day, so we put on his sailor collar (yes, I had themed accessories planned) and rented a paddle boat for the afternoon.

Many kayak rental companies in vacation towns are happy to rent to people planning to bring their dogs out on the water. Just be sure to give yourself extra time to familiarize your dog to the boat and to make sure that your dog isn't stressed by the boat. Small dogs tend to adjust more quickly to boating as they are already (generally) used to being picked up and carried, though there are many dogs who enjoy hitting the seas with their people. Increasingly, there are dog-friendly sail boating companies and other boating adventures available. After the paddle-boating, I took Mercury on a sunset sailboat trip in Cape Cod. There are also small ferry boats that can be dog friendly. In Cape Cod, I had the pleasure of taking both Mercury and my late dog Charlotte on a small shuttle boat out to Long Point.

Safety Note: Be sure to have appropriately sized life vests for your dogs before boating.

HAS YOUR DOG EVER BEEN ON A BOAT?

IF YES, WHAT KIND OF BOAT?

The next time you are on vacation or near water, think about researching different boat-rental options and explore if they are dog friendly!

RECORD WHAT YOUR DOG THINKS OF THE EXPERIENCE!

SNIFF WALK

Walking should be fun for you and your dog, it's an opportunity to explore the world together. Walks are, of course, great physical exercise for dogs (and us) but they also have the opportunity to be enriching. Unfortunately, in our busy world with cell phones and work schedules and errands that need to be run, sometimes walking the dog becomes just another chore, and the focus becomes getting from point A to point B as quickly and efficiently as possible. Sniffing is natural to our dogs; it's their most dominant sense and is stress relieving. Dogs have three hundred million scent receptors in their noses! As humans, we only have something like six million—dogs see the world through their nose more vibrantly than we can even imagine.

While there are some reasons you might need to keep a confined, quick speed while walking your dog (for example, if your dog is recovering from an orthopedic injury and you are working with a veterinary rehabilitation specialist), but if you are just on an average walk with your dog, it's important to let your dog pause, slow down, and sniff. Not all of us can accommodate an entirely sniffing-focused walk for every walk we take, but if you are taking your dog out for a walk, try to make sure to give them at least some time during the walk to sniff, if you do have to hurry your dog along, don't scold him for sniffing, redirect him back to you, treat, and praise. Having good leash manners is not at all incompatible with sniffing, and in fact, when dogs are permitted to sniff, to explore their world in a way that is most natural to them, your dog is significantly more likely to be responsive to training. Try to prioritize letting your dog have the opportunity to sniff. If you have a busy morning, try to leave for your walk a few minutes early to allow time for your dog to sniff, and make time for casual walks where you can give your dog as much time as she wants.

Spending more intentional and mindful time with our dogs is a great way to show them how important they are and to prioritize our relationship with our dog. In addition, try adding sniff-specific walks regularly. Can you manage a sniff walk once or twice a week?

TRACK WHERE YOU AND YOUR DOG WALK, AND THE DIFFERENT THINGS YOU NOTICE YOUR
DOG SMELLING:

Sniff Walk 1	Sniff Walk 2	Sniff Walk 3
Date _____	Date _____	Date _____
Observations:	Observations:	Observations:

Sniff Walk 4

Date _____

Observations:

_____

_____

_____

_____

_____

_____

_____

_____

_____

_____

_____

_____

Sniff Walk 5

Date _____

Observations:

_____

_____

_____

_____

_____

_____

_____

_____

_____

_____

_____

_____

Sniff Walk 6

Date _____

Observations:

_____

_____

_____

_____

_____

_____

_____

_____

_____

_____

_____

_____

WHAT WILL YOUR DOG FIND?

Dogs have a way of finding the most interesting things, sometimes even the sorts of things that we wouldn't notice. In this way, dogs can help us to be more aware of the world around us and more mindful and aware of the natural (and not so natural) world that surrounds us. Whether you and your dog are walking around a busy urban center or are out hiking in the wilderness, take notice of the things your dog is drawn to—it might surprise you what they find!

An abandoned shoe, the wing of a bird, a big stick, a deflated basketball, a pretty feather, a flower—there are so many interesting "treasures" to find just in your neighborhood!

WHAT ARE THINGS YOUR DOG IS DRAWN TO WHILE OUT ON A WALK? KEEP AN ONGOING RECORD OF THE DIFFERENT THINGS YOUR DOG IS EXCITED ABOUT: ARE THERE ANY COMMONALITIES OR THEMES?

PASTE ANY LEAVES OR SMALL/FLAT THINGS INTO THIS BOOK!

SURFING!

Your dog might like water, but can they surf? We've all seen the viral surfing dogs on the internet, but you'd be surprised how many dogs actually enjoy riding the waves—or at least floating. My senior Chihuahua mix doesn't have the stamina to swim that he once did (yes, my Chihuahua swims), and he can't swim as long or as far as my large dogs. As a bit of an accessibility aid, he started surfing on his shark-shaped float. The float we use was purchased online and originally designed for babies but works really well for my ten-pound dog. You can find dog-specific flotation devices for pools, or you can use surfboards and floats technically designed for people.

STARTING TO SURF

Safety first: Make sure that the float or surfboard you get for your dog is approved to support their weight. Also, be sure to expose your dog to the float or surfboard on land; we want to make sure that our dog is confident and comfortable with the flotation device before adding water into the mix. Be sure to be in the water with your dog when you do make the transition and whenever your dog is on the float. It's also a good idea to have a doggie life jacket for your dog, particularly if your dog isn't a strong swimmer.

DID YOUR DOG GIVE SURFING/FLOATING A CHANCE?

WHAT DID THEY THINK?

TAKE A CLASS!

There are so many wonderful things you and your dog can do together by yourselves, but sometimes you need, or want, a little extra help. Maybe you're trying to tackle a particular obedience skill, or perhaps you've always dreamed of learning how to play a particular sport. Working with a professional trainer and taking a class together is a wonderful opportunity not only to spend quality time with your dog but to grow your own and your dog's skills. Training dogs is partially about teaching the dog, but it's mostly about teaching us, the person, how to communicate with our dogs.

When looking for a class, regardless for what sport or for what issue, be sure to confirm that the trainer you're going to work with is a positive-reinforcement-based trainer, and that they do not use coercive or pain-based training methodologies. There is no universal certification for training dogs, anyone can call themselves a dog trainer, but not all dog trainers are created equal. Most cities and towns have a variety of dog trainers and sports classes available, but you can also take classes online! Online classes are a great option if you live in a rural community or if your dog is shy, reactive, or otherwise uncomfortable in a traditional class environment.

BACK TO SCHOOL!

CLASS NAME: _____

TRAINER: _____

DATES: _____

USE THIS SECTION TO TAKE NOTES FROM CLASS:

_____

_____

_____

_____

_____

_____

_____

_____

_____

_____

_____

_____

_____

_____

TAKE YOUR DOG ON A DATE

Our relationships with our dogs are some of the most important connections in our lives. Our dogs show up in our life daily, sometimes more frequently and more intensely than people are able to. Show your dog how much they mean to you by prioritizing spending quality time together as often as possible and even consider taking your dog on a date.

MAKE A LIST OF ANY DOG FRIENDLY RESTAURANTS OR LOCATIONS NEAR YOU:

_____

_____

_____

MAKE A LIST OF PLACES YOUR DOG ENJOYS GOING:

_____

_____

_____

PLAN THE DATE

If your dog is shy or not comfortable being around lots of dogs or people, make sure to plan your date to be a place that will be fun for your dog. For quiet dogs, a great alternative to going somewhere in public would be to pack a picnic for you and your dog and go to your favorite park or beach. You can visit pet shops, outdoor markets, hiking trails, or anywhere else your dog enjoys!

WHERE DID YOU GO? WHAT DID YOU DO?

SOCIAL MEDIA

Does your dog have more social-media followers than you? Mine does! No question, my dog is much cooler than I am. In all seriousness though, dogs are taking over the internet. Putting your dog online can be a fun opportunity to document your life together and the adventures that you go on. It's also a great way to meet other like-minded dog people and their dogs. Some dogs have even turned being social-media influencers or micro influencers into a little bit of a career!

WHAT SOCIAL MEDIA PLATFORMS IS YOUR DOG ALREADY ON?

Don't forget to use hashtags to find and connect with other dogs and so that other dogs can find your dog online! Hashtags include things like the city where you and your dog live, dogs of [insert name of your city or county], the breed of dog you have or your dog's mix, what you are doing together, dogs of [insert social media platform].

MAKE YOUR DOG A SOCIAL MEDIA PROFILE AND ADD OTHER DOG ACCOUNTS AS FRIENDS! KEEP NOTES ABOUT HOW MANY FOLLOWERS YOUR DOG HAS, WHAT OTHER DOGS YOU ADD AS FRIENDS, WHAT YOU LIKE AND DON'T LIKE ABOUT ENGAGING WITH OTHER DOGS ONLINE.

Have fun creating and managing online profiles for your dog but don't get too preoccupied with it. Make sure to spend quality time with your dog, don't just document them!

PLAN A DREAM VACATION WITH YOUR DOG

Is there somewhere you have always dreamed of traveling with your dog? Is it a real place? Is it reasonable? Some dream vacations might be doable, and some might be more fantastical for a variety of reasons—everything from your dog's size (flying a giant dog on vacation to Europe isn't always practical or safe), temperament (some dogs really are homebodies), and of course, finances—realistically we can't always afford the vacations we dream of, but that doesn't stop us from planning them!

Sometimes just planning a vacation is almost as fun as actually getting to go on it!

IF YOU COULD TRAVEL ANYWHERE WITH YOUR DOG, WHERE WOULD YOU GO (THIS CAN BE A REAL PLACE OR IMAGINED)? _____

_____

_____

_____

WHY DO YOU WANT TO TRAVEL THERE

_____

_____

_____

HOW WOULD YOU GET THERE

_____

WHAT WOULD YOU AND YOUR DOG DO THERE?

WHERE WOULD YOU STAY?

WHAT WOULD YOU EAT?

HOW LONG WOULD YOUR VACATION BE?

WHAT WOULD YOU BRING FOR YOUR DOG?

WHAT SOUVENIR WOULD YOUR DOG WANT TO BRING HOME?

WHAT WOULD YOUR DOG LIKE BEST ABOUT THE TRIP?

MAKE AN EMERGENCY KIT

None of us like to think about disasters striking, but unfortunately they are a scary part of our world. Natural disasters like hurricanes, forest fires, and earthquakes can impact anyone, and it's important to think of ways for you and your dog to be prepared. If a natural disaster were to strike your area, do you have everything your dog would need if you had to shelter in your home or if you had to evacuate?

EMERGENCY SUPPLY KIT

- Pet first-aid kit
- Food (enough to last at least a week)
- Bottled water
- Medication/supplements that your dog takes (at minimum a week's worth)
- ID tag attached to your dog's collar
- Leash
- Extra leash and collar just in case
- Blanket
- Collapsible food and water bowls
- Photo of your dog in case you were separated

OTHER SUPPLIES

_____

_____

_____

It's a good idea to keep print copies of vet records and any license and registration documents for your dog.

IMPORTANT INFORMATION

MY VET'S CONTACT INFORMATION:

_____

_____

_____

IF YOU HAD TO EVACUATE YOUR AREA, WHERE WOULD YOU WOULD GO?

_____

_____

_____

NAMES AND PHONE NUMBERS FOR PET FRIENDLY HOTELS IN THOSE AREAS:

_____

_____

_____

SHOPPING SPREE:
BUYING ANYTHING MY DOG TOUCHES

This is an activity that can either be an opportunity to spoil your dog or a chance for you and your dog to give back to dogs who are less fortunate by donating the spoils of your trip to a rescue group or shelter. This activity has become a bit of a meme online. The way it works is you take your dog to a pet store and commit to purchasing anything/everything your dog touches. It's completely ok (and probably a very good idea) to set a budget/limit on how much you are going to spend.

For extra fun you can bring a friend to video your dog picking out things in the store and upload it to your (or your dog's) social-media channels!

BEFORE YOU GO

WHAT KINDS OF THINGS DO YOU THINK YOUR DOG IS GOING TO PICK OUT AT THE PET SHOP?

SET A BUDGET:

AFTER YOU GO

HOW WAS THE SHOPPING SPREE? HOW DID YOUR DOG REACT?

WHAT DID YOUR DOG PICK OUT AT THE STORE?

DID ANYTHING YOUR DOG PICKED SURPRISE YOU?

DID YOU HAVE TO SAY NO TO EVERYTHING YOUR DOG SEEMED INTERESTED IN?

IF YOU DECIDED TO DONATE WHAT YOUR DOG PICKED OUT, WHERE DID YOU DONATE?

DID YOU STICK TO YOUR BUDGET?

SWIM!

Most dogs have a pretty natural attraction to the water, whether or not they are of a breed that was naturally bred to be in the water. Even dogs who might not be a fan of bath time or even walking in the rain are often pretty excited about being near bodies of water like lakes, rivers, and oceans. Bringing your dogs to play with and be near water.

WHAT DOES YOUR DOG THINK ABOUT WATER?

_____

_____

DOES YOUR DOG LIKE TO SWIM?

_____

_____

DOES YOUR DOG LIKE WADING?

_____

_____

DOES YOUR DOG CHASE WAVES?

_____

_____

_____

WHAT KIND OF OPPORTUNITIES FOR SWIMMING ARE NEAR YOU?

_____

_____

_____

If your dog isn't familiar with swimming or isn't confident, it's a really good idea to invest in a doggie life jacket that is approved for your dog's weight. This is especially important if you are thinking of taking your dog on some kind of boat ride, or if you have a heavier brachycephalic dog (one with a smooshy face). These dogs tend to struggle more with safe swimming. You want to always start slowly introducing your dog to water, making it fun and playful. Never force your dog to go into the water or to swim more than they are comfortable with.

If your dog is very uncomfortable with swimming, you might want to get some help from a professional. Many cities have doggie swim centers staffed by canine physical-rehabilitation specialists and/or swim instructors generally connected to the sport of dock diving (where dogs jump off docks and compete to see who can jump the farthest). A swim lesson is a great way to help your dog build confidence in the water, and will give you the skills required to support your dog while swimming.

Note: If you are swimming with your dog in natural water, be sure to check and follow local advisories about water safety. Especially in the late summer, there can be blue-green algae, which is toxic and deadly for dogs.

GIVING BACK

Most of our dogs are lucky enough to have pretty much everything they could want or need, but a lot of dogs in our communities aren't so lucky. These are dogs who might be in shelters and rescues, as well as dogs whose families might have fallen on hard times, or dogs living with people experiencing homelessness or struggling to pay their bills and keep kibble in the bowl! As we pamper our own dogs, it's nice to think about ways that we can give back to dogs struggling in our local community or even on our road.

Most communities have shelters and rescue groups, but does your community have a pet-food bank? Increasingly, organizations working with people experiencing homelessness are opening pet-food banks to provide dog food to animals living with unstably housed people or people living in poverty. These pet-food banks also often organize regular no-cost vet visits/clinics for participating members and their dogs so they can get appropriate medical care.

Search online for organizations providing support for homeless dogs or people experiencing homelessness with dogs, and find out what kind of support they need. Organizations like this often need volunteers as well as donations of dog food, dog treats, toys, blankets, and financial support.

ORGANIZATIONS IN YOUR AREA:

_____

_____

_____

WHAT ARE WAYS THAT YOU CAN SUPPORT THE ORGANIZATION WITH YOUR TIME OR
RESOURCES?

WHAT ARE WAYS YOU CAN INSPIRE FRIENDS, COLLEAGUES, FAMILY, ETC., TO SUPPORT
THIS AND OTHER ORGANIZATIONS?

WHERE TO GO? WHAT TO DO?

We all have those days where we want to do...something, but don't know what! For days like this, it can be helpful to have a list of things that you know you enjoy or even outings that you haven't gone on yet but want to explore with your dog.

FUN PLACES TO GO

This can include anything: walks, hikes, parks, pet shops, or any other pet-friendly establishments. You could even stop by your vet clinic or grooming shop for a quick hello and a treat to build more positive associations with these places and their staff.

MAKE A LIST OF THINGS YOU LIKE TO DO/PLACES YOU LIKE TO GO:

_____   _____
_____   _____
_____   _____
_____   _____
_____   _____

PLACES YOU'VE HEARD OF BUT HAVEN'T TRIED YET:

_____   _____
_____   _____
_____   _____
_____   _____
_____   _____

The next time you have a free afternoon without any plans and are looking for something fun to do with your dog, refer back to this list of outing ideas!

HIKING!

Hiking is a fantastic way to spend time in the outdoors with your dog! Hiking can be as laid back or as strenuous as you and your dog are up for. Many of us maybe didn't have a lot of exposure to things like hiking growing up, but dogs are wonderful at helping us learn to enjoy nature.

HIKING TIPS

Be sure to research ahead of time if the trail you are going on is dog friendly. Unfortunately, many hiking trails aren't welcoming to dogs, often either because of fragile environments or because other dog people have behaved badly in the past by not following leash laws, not scooping poop, etc.

Be honest with yourself about how strenuous of a hike you and your dog are up for. I love to hike with my dogs, but I'm not the most coordinated and honestly neither are my dogs; my youngest is a giant dog who has had reconstructive knee surgery, and my oldest is a super senior. I tend to look up reviews for trails online before heading out. I look for trails that are marked as good for beginners, and especially for trails that are good for young children. These trails tend to have wider paths, avoid steep drop offs (which makes me nervous for the safety of my dogs and myself), and generally have a more even footing.

If your dog is nervous or reactive around other dogs, be sure to check that the trails you are hiking require dogs to be leashed. This is the rule for most hiking areas, but some trails will permit off-leash dogs, so if your dog isn't social with other dogs, you'll want to avoid these areas. It's also a good idea to look for online reviews from other hikers with dogs to get a sense of how popular/busy the trail is likely to be. There are always going to be people that ruin areas for everyone by breaking leash laws; be prepared to be your dog's advocate and to call out ask for other pet owners to retrieve and leash their dogs.

BARK RANGER PROGRAM

In 2015, the US National Park Service began a "BARK Ranger" program for dogs (and their people). BARK stands for: Bag your dog's waste; Always use a leash; Respect wildlife, and; Know where you can go. Some parks have specialized collar tags and bandannas for your dog that you can purchase.

HIKING SUPPLIES

- Canine first aid kit
- Leash
- Collar or harness
- Updated identification tags (attached to your dog)
- Treats
- Portable water bowl
- Water for your dog
- Poop bags (bring extra)
- Cell phone

TRACK YOUR HIKING ADVENTURES—HAVE YOU AND YOUR DOG DISCOVERED SOMEWHERE GREAT? KEEP A RECORD OF THE PLACES YOU HIKE!

Date: _____

Trail: _____

Dog friendliness? _____

Review: _____

_____

_____

Date: _____

Trail: _____

Dog friendliness? _____

_____

Review: _____

_____

_____

Date: _____

Trail: _____

Dog friendliness? _____

_____

Review: _____

_____

_____

Date: _____

Trail: _____

Dog friendliness? _____

_____

Review: _____

_____

_____

Date: _____

Trail: _____

Dog friendliness? _____

_____

Review: _____

_____

_____

_____

_____

_____

DOGGIE CAFE!

More and more restaurants are incorporating dog-friendly patios into their business plans and restaurant designs, and some even have doggie menus! These present great opportunities to spend time with your dog and to turn an outing into a training opportunity to support and reward your dog for having good manners.

Before bringing your dog to a café, be sure to confirm that they are dog friendly; not all restaurants with outdoor dining areas are. Also find out if you can order from outside or if someone has to go inside to order. If it's the latter, be sure to bring someone with you who can go insider to order or stay outside with your dog. Never leave your dog tied outside a restaurant or store, even for a minute. Not only are they at risk of being dognapped, they are also at risk of being mistreated and harassed by passersby and other patrons of the restaurant, which can result in your dog being put into a dangerous or stressful situation.

Note: Be sure to consider whether your dog is the kind that is comfortable around other dogs and people. There is no shame in admitting that this is the kind of situation that would be upsetting or stressful for your dog. Many dogs aren't comfortable in public places where they will be in close proximity or have to engage with people and other dogs. If your dog would prefer to have more space, it's best to get takeout and enjoy your meal together at home!

RESTAURANT REVIEWS

Name: ....

Review: ....

Name:

Review:

Name:

Review:

Name:

Review:

Name:

Review:

Name:

Review:

Name:

Review:

Name:

Review:

SPORTS!

ORBIT

For this trick, your dog will circle backwards around you. This is a really fun skill, and an impressive trick that is fun for your dog while being a great way to impress family and friends, and it's also a great trick to incorporate into other skills, like dancing with your dog.

INSTRUCTIONS

1. Have treats in both hands. Ask your dog to line up next to you on your left side if they know how to do that, or use your treat to lure your dog next to you. Orbiting is a little bit easier to teach large dogs, because it involves less bending for the handler, but it's a trick that dogs of any size can do.

2. With the treat, lure your dog backwards and move them slightly out away from your body. With your dog's nose on the treat, your dog will move the opposite direction and begin to curve around behind you. This is the point where you need to be a little bit flexible as you move your dog behind you.

3. Bring your right hand (which also has a treat in it) behind your back and put it on your dog's nose (you can give your dog the treat in your left hand at this point).

4. Keeping your dog's nose on the treat, bring them fully around your body, and as your dog comes parallel with you, pull your hand away from your body which will pivot your dog again to finish the circle in front of you.

5. This trick requires your dog to move a lot, so don't be afraid to go slowly. Going slowly early on will assist your dog with understanding. You may also want to use a treat like string cheese where you can pinch off little bits of it as your dog follows

your hand/the treat around your body. It can help to start this trick near a corner of your room, which will inspire your dog to move in the right directions.

6. Repeat this multiple times over several sessions, continuing to lure your dog. As your dog begins to anticipate the movement, add in your choice of verbal cues: "circle," "orbit," and "around" are all good cues, but of course you can call this trick anything. As your dog gets more confident, you can begin to replace the lure with smaller and smaller physical gestures in combination with the verbal cue. When your dog is successful, give them lots of treats and praise!

With a little bit of practice your dog will be ready to "orbit" anywhere!

PARKOUR

You've probably seen the viral videos of people jumping over walls, scaling trees—that's parkour, essentially turning the world into your private jungle gym. While most of us aren't going to go out and scale walls anytime soon, the sport/activity of canine parkour might be more interesting to you and your dog. Parkour for dogs involves jumping, balancing, climbing, and is essentially a form of urban agility through which dogs are able to learn safe ways to engage with their environments.

I got very excited about parkour-related skills before I even knew that there was a word for them or that this was something other people were doing. Living in NYC at the time, with a very reactive and anxious dog (but one who loved to walk), parkour-like skills became an informal way for my dog Charlotte and I to explore our neighborhood while keeping her stress levels down and developing muscle tone, confidence, and agility. Parkour games are directly tied to all the habits we have been working on in this book: being more intentional with the time that we spend with our dogs, and playing close attention to the world around us. When you are out with your dog, whether you are on a beach, in a park, on a hiking trail, or on a city sidewalk, keep your eyes open for aspects of the environment that you and your dog could engage with. Be on the lookout for things your dog can partially or completely climb onto, climb over, go under, go around, or go through. Not only are parkour games a lot of fun for dogs, they also provide great opportunities to set your dog up for some cute pictures to post on your social media, posing with all the fun things you find!

Parkour has even become a competitive sport in which you and your dog can work together to earn titles that demonstrate your dog's skills anywhere in the world! Learn more about these organizations and the ways you can record videos of your dog's adventures to earn titles through these two organizations (they each have different regulations and specifications):

International Dog Parkour Association: www.DogParkour.org
All Dogs Parkour: www.AllDogsParkour.com

AGILITY

Agility is a high-octane sport in which dogs sail over jumps, weave between poles, zip through tunnels, and climb over obstacles. Agility is a lot of fun and is a very fast-paced, very competitive sport. It's not for everyone, but if you are looking for something fun to do with your dog, you can create your own mini agility course for your dog in your home or yard.

Footing is extremely important to think about. Make sure that you aren't asking your dog to run or jump on slippery floors like hardwood or tile. Similarly, you want to avoid all hard surfaces, like concrete, because they can easily cause injury to your dog's joints. Beyond that, have a lot of fun building and finding things for your dog to walk on, jump over, or go under, and then create a little sequence, putting a few obstacles near each other and guiding your dog (don't forget treats!) through your mini course. In your living room, this might mean creating a jump out of a broomstick propped up on some books, arranging a low ottoman that your dog can get up onto and do some tricks on before continuing on to another book jump, and then perhaps a tunnel made out of boxes! If you have a yard, you can spread out a little bit more and create a small obstacle course, and if you are a little bit handy (or you know someone who is), you can find instructions online for building "contact equipment" like a-frames and dog walks. For at-home play, you want to look for "teacup"-size equipment that is lower to the ground and safer for a wider range of dogs and for training without a professional instructor. Remember to start slow, with lots of praise and encouragement, and if your dog is ever nervous or uncomfortable, that's a cue to back up in order to ensure your dog stays happy and comfortable with the game.

DOODLE AND DESCRIBE THE "AGILITY" COURSES THAT YOU HAVE CREATED FOR YOUR DOG BELOW!

WHAT DID YOUR DOG THINK ABOUT YOUR AT-HOME AGILITY COURSES?

_____

_____

_____

UNDER!

Teaching your dog to go "under" objects is a useful skill to have, and is one more way that you can teach your dog to engage with objects in their environment. It's also a useful skill if you are out exploring and hiking or even in a more urban setting if you've stopped at a dog-friendly café. Teaching your dog that it's safe to duck under objects comes in handy frequently! This is a skill that smaller dogs tend to excel at because of their size; they are already used to being expected to move under objects. Big dogs absolutely can learn this skill, and in fact it's really good for them, but it may take them a little longer to feel comfortable with it.

You can start training at home or out in the world in an area where your dog is comfortable. Start with a setup where your dog has to go under something but doesn't need to duck their head. Either lure them under or toss a treat, and when your dog passes under and gets the treat, give them lots of praise.

When your dog is comfortable with something over their head, it's time to move onto asking them to go under something where they need to slightly duck their head. You can find this kind of natural setup or you can create it at home with a broomstick spread between chairs or stools in your home or yard. Just make sure whatever your dog is passing under is secured so it won't fall if your dog's head touches it. Again, toss a treat under and when your dog goes for the treat, give them lots of praise.

At this point, do a few repetitions and begin to introduce your verbal cue: "under," "duck," or "crouch" are all good verbal cues that work well for this skill.

The more times you practice, the greater the diversity of things you can work with your dog to go under! Start to slowly decrease the height of things you are asking your dog to go under. Remember that as the items get lower, your dog will have to use different muscles and will need to build up those muscles to be able to do it.

How many different things can you find for your dog to (safely) go under?

Signs, fences, benches, bike racks, stable fallen logs, etc., are all great items with which to practice this skill.

WHAT DID YOU FIND FOR YOUR DOG TO GO UNDER?

OBEDIENCE SKILLS

"Obedience" sounds boring and stuffy, or at worst coercive, but in the dog world it's actually a really fun sport and a way to work with your dog. Practicing obedience skills can increase your dog's bond with you, and increase your ability to communicate with each other!

One of the big keys to teaching any obedience skill, from "sit" and "down" to walking calmly next to you, is patience; working at your dog's pace, setting your dog up to succeed, and training with positive reinforcement. If your dog does something you don't like or isn't successful, it's just a sign that your dog was pushed beyond their skill set at that moment or put "over their threshold," meaning they were too distracted or overwhelmed, and so they weren't mentally capable of focusing in the way that you were asking them to. The key to mastering obedience skills with your dog is patience, patience, patience, and a whole lot of high-value treats! We want as much as possible to set our dogs up for success and to inspire our dogs to see us as much more exciting and enriching than the world around us, meaning that we are exciting, fun, playful, we have treats, and are the source of very exciting games.

WHAT ARE YOUR OBEDIENCE GOALS FOR YOUR DOG?

_____

_____

_____

If you and your dog hit a training wall and get overwhelmed or stuck, it's a great time to pull in some professional help with a positive-reinforcement–based trainer. Working with a dog trainer is not a sign of failure. We all need a little bit of help sometimes with finding new ways to communicate with our dogs.

TUNNELS

Most (though not all) dogs enjoy going through tunnels. For some dogs of terrier descent, going into tunnels is very natural, and for a lot of other dogs, it's just a whole lot of fun! For dogs that train and compete in agility, there is a term, "tunnel suck," which refers to when dogs get distracted by tunnels even when it's not the obstacle they are supposed to tackle next! You don't have to have a lot of fancy equipment for your dog to enjoy tunnels, it's actually something that you can make at home for your dog to enjoy.

SUPPLIES

Boxes or blankets and chairs. The easiest way to make a tunnel is by using a large box, opened on both ends. The size of box you need will depend on the size of dog that you have. You can also create a tunnel with blankets propped up on furniture to create a space for dogs to go under!

PURCHASING

If you aren't feeling crafty, you can also purchase a kid's play tunnel at most toy stores or big-box retailers fairly inexpensively. If you have a small or even medium-sized dog, this will work pretty well, but if you have a large dog you are going to need something a little...larger. Twenty-four inches in diameter is the standard for competitive agility tunnels, which is a good size to keep in mind if you have a larger dog, as even the biggest of dogs (including my Newfoundland!) can generally crouch down to fit through a tunnel of this size. Competition-strength tunnels are going to be very expensive, but there are cheaper practice versions that work reasonably well if you are just playing around at home with your dog.

When you show your dog your tunnel, either purchased or handmade, it's a good idea to have another person to help you. Have your helper (someone your dog is comfortable with) hold your dog on one side of the tunnel, then go to the other side and put your face down into the tunnel and call your dog's name to get their attention. When your dog is looking at you, have your helper let go of your dog and continue to call your dog through the tunnel, offering lots of praise and treats when your dog gets to you. After a few repetitions you can start sending your dog through the tunnel without your helper, but make sure to keep the praise and treats coming!

WHAT KIND OF TUNNEL DID YOU FIND OR MAKE FOR YOUR DOG?

_____

_____

_____

WHAT DID YOUR DOG THINK OF IT?

_____

_____

_____

GO AROUND/BARREL-RACING GAME

Does your dog want to be a rodeo star? Teaching your dog to go around objects is a fun challenge.

INSTRUCTIONS

1. Start inside or in an area with few distractions. Take an object: you can use anything like a flowerpot, a box, or a two-liter soda bottle filled with water or sand for weight, or even just a backpack standing up. The object you want to use will depend on your dog's size; when first teaching, you want to pick something that your dog can't easily knock over if they bump into it. This is especially important if your dog is nervous about noises or objects moving. Eventually your dog will be able to differentiate and "go around" any object.

2. Have treats that are high value for your dog.

3. Keep the treat on your dog's nose and walk them towards the object you want them to go around. Guide them around the object.

4. As they complete a circle, praise them and give your dog the treat.

5. Start introducing the verbal cue (examples include: "circle," "rodeo," and "around") while continuing to lure your dog with a treat.

6. After a couple of sessions, you can begin to fade the lure by giving the verbal cue first as your dog is looking at the object. If your dog goes around, give them lots of

praise and treats. If your dog doesn't quite have it, you can move in with your lure and help them out.

As you are teaching, be sure to begin introducing your dog to different objects you want them to circle around. The better your dog gets, the more you can start adding distance. Go slowly while adding distance. Back up one step at a time until you can send your dog away from you to circle an object as you stay further away.

Continue rehearsing in your home and in areas with few distractions, and then start practicing in more distracting areas like in the park or on your walk. When you start to practice this activity in a new area, you'll want to lower the criteria by staying closer to the object you are asking your dog to circle.

How many things can you find for your dog to go around? Trees, telephone poles, playground equipment, and rocks are all easy-to-find objects your dog can circle. Start incorporating "go arounds" into your on-the-go training, and record the different things you've found for your dog to rodeo around!

Note: When you start practicing this trick in public spaces, it's great to use a long line (a longer than normal leash) if the area is safe and your dog is comfortable on one. It's important to respect leash laws and not let your dog off-leash for this activity.

EXTRA CREDIT

You can use a different verbal cue for circling around an object to the left or circling to the right. Teach the opposite direction the same way that you started teaching the first time. Once your dog is confident circling an object in either direction, you're ready to take your rodeo on the road!

WHAT OBJECTS CAN YOU FIND FOR YOUR DOG TO GO AROUND?

_____

_____

_____

_____

_____

_____

_____

CANINE GOOD CITIZEN

The American Kennel Club's CGC or Canine Good Citizen program is a perfect introduction to competition obedience and obedience training for any dog. Any breed or mixed breed of dog can participate in the CGC testing program, and it's not only a good way to test your dog's general polite obedience skills, it's also a good way to get a taste for competition obedience and to see if it's something that you and your dog might enjoy together. The categories you want to train for that will be included in the CGC exam are:

1. Accepting a friendly stranger.

2. Sitting politely for petting.

3. Being clean and well groomed.

4. Walking on a loose leash.

5. Walking through a crowd without getting distracted.

6. "Sit" and "Down" and staying on cue.

7. Coming when called.

8. Staying neutral, happy, and in control when greeting another dog.

9. Not reacting to a distraction.

10. Supervised separation during which the dog stays with the evaluator while the handler stays out of sight for a few minutes.

CGC testing can take place privately, working with a CGC evaluator certified by the AKC, or alternatively, most AKC dog shows will offer CGC testing for which you can either sign up in advance or sometimes on day of the show. Since the program started in 1989, more than one million dogs have earned their CGC title! Could your dog be next? Even if you aren't interested in pursuing the CGC program with your dog, the skills involved in the test are a good framework to use when setting training goals and structuring your plans with your dog.

For more information and to find a CGC evaluator near you visit www.AKC.org.

Note: There are many, many wonderful dogs, including rescue dogs with past trauma and dogs with limited socialization in puppyhood, who, for whatever reason, are never going to be candidates to take the CGC exam. Perhaps because they are triggered by being in close proximity to other dogs or are uncomfortable being approached by people. I've had these dogs! This does not in any way mean these dogs are "bad citizens" or that they aren't deserving of or can't enjoy and benefit from obedience training.

WALKING LEG WEAVES

This is a fun skill for your dog that is very impressive for your friends and family to watch, and can also be a skill that comes in handy for activities like musical freestyle.

LEG WEAVES

Start teaching this trick in a stationary position with your legs spread apart. Take a treat that your dog is excited about. Have treats in both hands and lure your dog between your legs, then reach behind you with your other hand and lure your dog around. When she comes through your leg and around the side of your body, give the treat and praise them! After a few repetitions you can start introducing a verbal cue ("weave," or "eight," or any cue of your choice), and you can begin fading out the lure with treats into a smaller physical cue, rewarding your dog at the end.

When your dog is a pro at weaving in figure eights between your legs, you can expand into an impressive movement-based trick where your dog will weave through your legs as you walk forward. Start by practicing the stationary-leg weave a few times.

1.   With treats in both hands again, give your dog the cue for your figure eight, and as your dog wraps around your first leg, take one small step forward with your other leg so that, as your dog wraps around, they are now positioned to go around the front leg, then treat and praise them.

2.   Next try again with two steps, again having treats in both hands to lure/ support your dog.

As you are teaching, you will want to be thoughtful about your steps, making sure that you pause / hesitate after each step so that your dog has a chance to get through your legs without being stepped on.

    🐕   As you and your dog get more experienced and practiced, you can fade the lure by asking your dog to weave more steps before treating, but keep the verbal praise up and make sure to treat after a few steps and each time vary how many steps you ask your dog to leave before treating. You can also make your movements more fluid with fewer hesitations as your dog becomes more confident.

BETWEEN

Teaching your dog to walk between two close objects is a skill that is useful for playing around with parkour, and is a fun way to enrich your walks. When teaching this skill, start with obstacles that you and your dog can walk between together. If your dog is nervous, have a treat you can lure/lead them through with and start with two objects close together, but not very long (so two trees vs. two retaining walls).

When your dog is comfortable going between objects with you, you can place them on one side of the obstacle, pass the leash between (feel free to use a long line for added length if it's safe to do so in the area you are in: away from cars, roads, and where it won't interfere with others' enjoyment of the park), and call them through. When they're confident, you can start introducing a verbal cue: "between" is a common one. Walking between objects that are close together is a great confidence-building skill for dogs and can come in handy when you are out exploring or hiking together.

WHAT KINDS OF THINGS CAN YOU FIND FOR YOUR DOG TO WALK BETWEEN WITH YOU?

_____

_____

_____

WHAT THINGS CAN YOU FIND FOR YOU DOG TO WALK BETWEEN WITHOUT YOU?

_____

_____

_____

EXTRA CREDIT

ASK YOUR DOG TO BACK UP IN A NARROW SPACE NEXT TO YOU. WHAT AREAS WERE YOU ABLE TO WORK ON BACKING UP IN?

_____

_____

_____

_____

_____

_____

TRICKY FOOTING

Regardless of whether you are socializing a new puppy or working with your older dog, it's important to get them used to walking on a wide diversity of footing. Ideally this is something you will expose your dog to as a puppy, but it's never too late to support your dog gaining experience and confidence with new challenges. Some dogs aren't at all concerned about walking on any surface, but a lot of dogs are less confident, especially with metal, raised surfaces, and/or surfaces that move.

Walk your dog on a diversity of surfaces, and when confident/comfortable, start to do tricks or other behaviors on those novel surfaces. Finding different surfaces to expose your dog to can be as easy as setting up things you might have around the house (like foam matting and plywood) or as involved as going on a scavenger hunt in your neighborhood or on outings looking for different surfaces. When you find a new surface to expose your dog to, you can lure them on with treats, or even better, put a few treats onto the new surface and ask your dog to get them. If your dog is afraid, never force them onto a new surface; rather, allow them to make a choice of when and how to engage. We want to keep this fun and successful for our dogs. You can find interesting surfaces everywhere, from forest trails to city streets. Parks and specifically children's playgrounds can provide a lot of great, enriching surfaces to explore, just remember to be considerate and not approach the playground if there are children present.

Safety Note: Be sure that any object/surface you are asking your dog to walk onto is low to the ground and stable enough to support the weight of your dog. With unsteady or wobbly things, be extra careful to ensure that the object is low to the ground in case your dog gets spooked and tries to jump off so they won't get hurt. If you are showing your dog an object that moves or might be unsteady, be sure to show your dog the movement before asking them to get on, otherwise you're likely to end up getting your dog confidently onto the object which will then move, and your dog will be very reluctant to approach it again and may become wary about other surfaces in the future. Also, remember that dogs are situational learners, and your dog might be comfortable with a novel surface in one environment but still might be nervous about it somewhere else, so always approach new surfaces prepared to support your dog.

HOW MANY SURFACES CAN YOU FIND TO EXPOSE YOUR DOG TO? CHALLENGE YOURSELF TO FIND AS MANY AS POSSIBLE, AND RECORD WHAT YOUR DOG THINKS!

Surface _____   Surface _____
Dog Reaction _____   Dog Reaction _____

Surface _____   Surface _____
Dog Reaction _____   Dog Reaction _____

Surface _____   Surface _____
Dog Reaction _____   Dog Reaction _____

Surface _____   Surface _____
Dog Reaction _____   Dog Reaction _____

Surface _____   Surface _____
Dog Reaction _____   Dog Reaction _____

Surface _____   Surface _____
Dog Reaction _____   Dog Reaction _____

Surface _____   Surface _____
Dog Reaction _____   Dog Reaction _____

WALK THE PLANK!

Ok, no, we aren't going to play pirates, but we can teach our dog to walk along a platform! This skill takes a lot of coordination and can be a great confidence boost for dogs. It's also a great way to prepare your dog for sports like canine parkour and dog agility.

Approach teaching "Walk the Plank" in a similar way to "Four-On" (see page 220). Start with planks/objects that are a bit wider than your dog; eventually you can work down to narrower planks, but that takes increased confidence and coordination, so you want to go slowly to keep your dog confident and successful.

Safety Note: Make sure that everything you ask your dog to walk on is at a safe and low height. It's better to have your dog on a supportive back-clip harness than on a collar, front-clip, or head halter in case your dog jerks suddenly or jumps off the plank unexpectedly. Also, be sure that the surface your dog is jumping down onto isn't concrete or another hard surface

Depending on the size of your dog, logs, boards of wood balanced on bricks or cinder blocks, or picnic-table benches are all great planks for your dog to explore.

WHAT PLANKS DID YOU FIND FOR YOUR DOG TO WALK ALONG?

_____   _____

_____   _____

_____   _____

_____   _____

_____   _____

_____   _____

_____   _____

_____   _____

_____   _____

_____   _____

DIY WEAVE POLES

If you have ever seen a dog-agility competition online, on TV, or in person, you were probably impressed with the skill of those dogs, especially when they slalomed through those weave poles! You can teach these skills at home with very simple supplies.

To make your own weave poles at home you can use anything from toilet plungers (new ones please!) to sticks or PVC pipe stuck in the ground. You can also inexpensively find small plastic cones (dollar stores and dollar sections are your friend!). Set up your DIY weave poles with twenty-four inches of spacing between the poles—this is generally the standard distance.

There are *lots* of ways to teach dogs to weave, especially if you are training a dog you hope to compete in agility with. The easiest and fastest way to teach weaving for play is by luring your dog through the poles with a treat. When you lure your dog through, you want your dog to enter with their left shoulder closest to the pole (this doesn't matter if you are just playing at home, but if you ever want to translate this to agility, it's a good habit for you and your dog to get into).

Be patient with yourself and your dog as you teach weaving—it's one of the most complicated skills in agility, and it will probably take your dog a little while to get the hang of the activity.

WHAT DID YOU USE TO MAKE WEAVE POLES WITH?

HOW IS WEAVE-POLE TRAINING GOING?

_____

_____

_____

_____

DANCING

Musical freestyle, also known as dancing with dogs, is a fast-growing sport where people and dogs come together to literally dance! No, dogs who dance don't (usually) actually get into the music themselves; the sport is set to music and dog and handler perform a choreographed routine linking together tricks like spins and leg weaves and pairing it with music! The tricks are generally linked together with traditional obedience heeling, which is part of what gives it the look of dogs and people actually dancing together.

Musical freestyle is a sport that is a lot of fun for audiences to watch, but it can also be a profoundly private sport in which you compete via video submission, or never at all and just have a lot of fun with your dog. The sport, like any dance routine, is about the chemistry and connection between dog and handler. The goal is to seamlessly cue your dog. In competition at the higher levels, dogs must respond only to verbal cues or physical cues that are smoothly integrated into the routine. The idea is to make it look like you and your dog are spontaneously breaking into dance, not like you have practiced a routine together. Many musical freestyle routines feel almost like musical theater, with a story connected to the song being acted out by dog and handler through the dance. Musical freestyle does require a lot of practice though, the goal again being establishing a connection between you and your doggie "dance partner."

SOME TRICKS THAT WORK REALLY WELL IN MUSICAL FREESTYLE INCLUDE:

- 🦴 Spins;
- 🦴 Heeling;
- 🦴 Having your dog spin forwards around you;
- 🦴 Having your dog go around you backwards, or "orbiting" (taught on page 159);
- 🦴 Having your dog "kick" your feet with their front paws;

- Having your dog weaving through your legs with you stationary or walking (taught on page 182).

But you can choreograph in any tricks your dog enjoys!

JUMPING

Jumping is a fun skill that comes naturally to most dogs! Jumping is a key component in a lot of sports, from agility to obedience, and is a lot of fun for our dogs.

INSTRUCTIONS

In order to teach your dog to jump, you want to have treats or a toy they are excited about.

1. Set them up directly in front of the jump obstacle.

2. When your dog looks over the jump, toss the toy or treat. Our goal is for the dog to not see us tossing the treat because, for safety reasons, when they jump we want our dog looking at where they are going and not at us.

3. After a few repetitions, add in your verbal cue of choice.

Safety Note: Because jumping is a high impact activity, it's a good idea to get clearance from your vet before asking your dog to jump. Puppies and young dogs should never be allowed or encouraged to jump, as it can harm their developing joints and lead to lifelong orthopedic injuries. The larger the dog, the slower they will develop and the longer you need to wait before asking your dog to jump.

FOOTING

It's important that we not ask our dogs to jump on hard or slippery surfaces. Avoid asking your dog to jump on concrete, hardwood, tile, or linoleum floors.

HEIGHTS

Make sure all of your jumps are sized appropriately for your dog. The goal should never be to try and see how high our dogs can jump.

AMERICAN KENNEL CLUB
AGILITY JUMP HEIGHTS

For agility and other dog sports, jump heights are based on a dog's height at the withers (shoulder blades).

JUMP HEIGHTS

- Dogs 11 inches and under at the withers jump 8 inches.
- Dogs 14 inches and under at the withers jump 12 inches.
- Dogs 18 inches and under at the withers jump 16 inches.
- Dogs 22 inches and under at the withers jump 20 inches.
- Dogs over 22 inches at the withers jump 24 inches.

ACTIVITY

Make an agility jump by balancing a PVC pipe, pool noodle, or dowel on bricks or boxes in your house or yard. When you're out on walks, look for natural jumps like partially downed logs to ask your dog to jump.

WHAT JUMPS DID YOU MAKE?

WHAT NATURAL JUMPS DID YOU FIND?

DID YOU PUT SEVERAL JUMPS TOGETHER INTO A "JUMPERS" COURSE? IF SO, DOODLE YOUR COURSE BELOW.

TREIBBALL

Treibball is a growing competitive sport that is essentially urban herding. This sport enables dogs to learn and practice herding skills just like real sheepdogs, but without the need for any livestock! Instead of animals, dogs herd large exercise or Pilates-style balls, which can be ordered online fairly inexpensively. For working on the beginning stages of this trick at home, you can use any large playground ball.

In the sport of Treibball, dogs are sent out behind a "flock" of balls. The dog and handler work as a team like a shepherd and herding dog would. The dog is working at a distance and pushes balls at the handler's direction into a goal. To play this game at home, we are going to start with "shaping" (taught on page 72) to help our dog figure out what we want.

INSTRUCTIONS

1. Start with one ball and a lot of treats that your dog likes.

2. Put the ball in front of your dog and reward your dog for being near the ball or showing any interest in the ball.

3. When your dog's nose hits the ball because they sniff it, give them lots of treats and praise.

4. Because sniffing/touching the ball with her nose is what got treats, your dog is going to repeat the behavior. Each time she does, praise/click and treat.

5. When your dog is constantly touching the ball, start to increase the criteria before the rewards; we want our dog to be pushing the ball—you'd be surprised, even a very

large dog can very gently touch the ball and keep it from moving. What we want for treibball is good strong pushes.

6. When your dog is pushing the ball, you can add in your verbal cue: "push," "ball," and "soccer" are all good cues, but you can use anything you want.

7. We want our dog to push the ball towards us, so I recommend starting to teach with the ball between you and your dog, which will make it easier later to start adding distance.

8. As your dog gets more experience with the game, you can start asking for multiple pushes before you reward with a treat.

9. Buy or create a "goal." You can find inexpensive ones for kids at dollar stores, or you can create one with cones or boxes. Essentially you just want to create a goal area where you can direct your dog to push the ball into.

10. For sending your dog out, this is a great time to brush up on or teach your dog the skill. Put out a target—anything relatively flat: a piece of cardboard, a coaster, a yogurt lid. Yes, you can use this book—and praise/click and reward your dog anytime they touch the target with their foot. When your dog has been successful, add in your verbal cue of choice: "target," "place," "hit it," etc.

11. When your dog is solid at targeting, try putting the ball near the target and asking your dog to target—this might be harder, because the ball will be a distraction. If your dog goes for the ball instead of the target, just make the exercise simpler, putting yourself between the ball and the target or moving the ball farther way.

12. When your dog is happily going to the target near the ball, position your treibball course with yourself in the goal area, the target past the ball, and the ball between you and your dog.

13. Send your dog to the target and then ask them to "push" the ball towards you until the ball goes into the goal area.

EXTRA CREDIT

Add more than one ball! Add balls slowly and make sure your dog is able to concentrate on one ball at a time.

If you want to learn more about Treibball and how to get involved in the sport for real, check out resources from The American Treibball Association at www. AmericanTreibballAssociation.org.

GAMES & CHALLENGES

DETECTION-DOG GAME

Scent work is one of the fastest growing dog sports. This sport is a civilian version of the kind of detection work that military, police, and search and rescue dogs do. For this sport, the dog is in charge and the handler has to completely trust them to alert to the designated odor. In scent work, trial dogs are looking for specific essential-oil scents (Birch, Anise, Clove, and Cypress). When teaching dogs the basics of scent work, you initially want to pair the scent the dog is looking for with a "primary odor," a.k.a. food! A fun and easy entry-level game you and your dog can play at home involves your dog exercising her nose to search for the primary odor.

INSTRUCTIONS

1. Save empty delivery boxes and other boxes that you find.

2. Scatter the boxes around a room, leaving them open at first, and drop treats into some of the boxes.

3. Show your dog the boxes and invite them to search!

4. Every time your dog finds food in a box, praise them as they eat the treats and encourage them to keep looking. When they've found the last treat, praise, call them, and give another treat.

ADVANCED GAMES

- Change the order/arrangement of the boxes each time.

- Don't put the box(es) with the treats in the same location each time. This will make sure your dog isn't memorizing a pattern and is instead using their nose to find the hidden treats.
- Close the boxes, and when your dog noses at the correct box where the treats are hidden, praise them and immediately open the box.

THIRTY-DAY PAWS-UP CHALLENGE

One of my favorite ways to build confidence in dogs is by setting fun training challenges. This also helps your dog build and strengthen their muscles and helps to develop coordination. Putting their paws up onto things on cue is also great for photos!

INSTRUCTIONS

1. Start in an area with few distractions, like at home or in your yard. Have some high-value treats and show your dog the object that you would like them to put their paws up onto.

2. Show your dog the treat in your hand and lure your dog forward towards the object. Encourage them to put their feet up onto the object.

3. As soon as your dog's feet touch the object, praise/click and treat.

4. Repeat several times, and when your dog is confidently putting their front feet onto the box, start to introduce your verbal cue of choice: "paws up," "two," and "on" are all great choices. Introduce the verbal cue when your dog is moving towards the object, right before their feet touch.

5. When your dog is confident with putting their front paws onto the object in a low-distraction environment, you can start to phase out your lure. Keep using your high-value treats, and ask your dog to put their paws up on an object with your verbal cue. When they do, praise/click and treat!

6. Dogs aren't usually very good at generalizing, so having taught this behavior at home, you may need to back up a little bit and use some luring when you first start to do

paws-up tricks out in the world. Keeping an eye out for ways that you and your dog can incorporate their environment is a fun way to enrich your walks, and is also a good way to prep you and your dog for the fun, environmentally-involved sport of parkour.

TAKE THE CHALLENGE!

Are you and your dog ready for the paws-up challenge? For the next thirty days, can you and your dog find a new (safe) object each day to put their feet up onto? Get creative! Rocks, signs, picnic tables, playground equipment, tires, and logs all make great obstacles. Just be sure to follow all leash laws and respect private property as well as sacred spaces like cemeteries.

KEEP TRACK OF ALL THE OBSTACLES YOU FIND FOR YOUR DOG TO PRACTICE "PAWS UP"

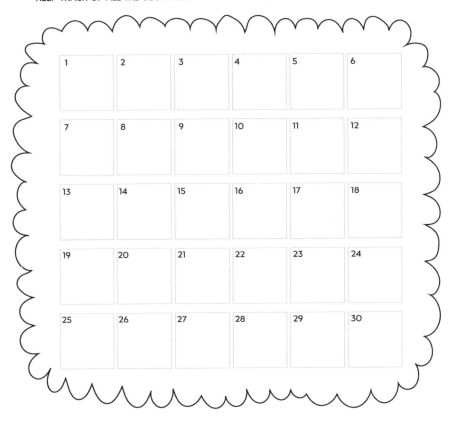

HIDE & SEEK

Hide and seek isn't just a fun game for kids, it's actually a fantastic game to play with your dog! Hide and seek can be played in even the smallest of apartments, or spread out if you have a larger house! It's also an enriching game that gets your dog moving and is very mentally stimulating. To play the game, you'll want to leave your dog in one room or area of your house. If your dog has a solid "stay," you can leave them in a stay position, or you can wait until your dog is occupied and then sneak out of the room.

When you first start playing the game, don't hide too well, just begin by going into another room or area of your home and calling your dog. When your dog finds you, give them lots of praise and have a little party together. The more experience with the game your dog has, the more difficult you can make your hiding places. Try crouching behind a piece of furniture or behind the back of an opened door. Just make sure that wherever you hide is somewhere that your dog can actually find/get to, so for example, don't close yourself into a closet; we want our dogs to be successful! Anytime your dog finds you, be sure to give them lots of praise and play together. If your dog enjoys toys, have a favorite toy with you and play with it when your dog finds you!

If at any point your dog is taking a long time to find your or seems lost, you can call again to give your dog a little extra help getting to you!

RECORD YOUR HIDE-AND-SEEK ADVENTURES WITH YOUR DOG—WHERE DID YOU HIDE? DID YOUR DOG FIND YOU? HOW LONG DID IT TAKE YOUR DOG TO FIND YOU?

BOX GAME

You don't need to have any kind of fancy training equipment to train and enrich your dog's life. In fact, some of our best training opportunities can arise with simple supplies you can find around your house. Some of my favorite training props are boxes—especially the heavy cardboard boxes that are used for deliveries. Most of us get regular deliveries of various things. Usually those boxes just go into recycling, but you can actually use them to train your dog first and have a lot of fun with them!

Depending on the size of your dog and the size of the boxes, you can use them in a variety of ways. You can turn small boxes on their side to create small jumps and hurdles (don't forget to keep jump heights low and on good footing, like carpet, for safety). You can put two boxes parallel to each other and ask your dog to go between the boxes, and then you and your dog can play the box challenge! For this game we will be seeing how many different things you and your dog can figure out to do with a box! I prefer a sturdy and decently sized box. Have some treats handy and see how many things you can ask your dog to do with a box!

HOW MANY THINGS CAN YOUR DOG DO WITH A BOX (PAWS IN, FRONT FEET IN, BACK FEET IN, ALL FEET IN, TWO PAWS ON, ALL PAWS ON)?

A GAME A DAY

Between our jobs, social media, and relationships with other people, sometimes without meaning to, our relationship with our dog can take a little bit of a backseat. I think it's always good to take a step back from all the things that distract, excite, and stress us out to remember that we are the whole world to our dogs; we control everything from when they eat to when they get to go outside. When we're away, our dogs wait eagerly for our return, and greet us exuberantly whenever we return, whether we've been gone for five minutes or five hours.

What kinds of games does your dog most like to play? Chase? Fetch? Tug? Playing is not only a wonderful way to bond with your dog, but the play is also good for your dog's physical well-being. It promotes increased flexibility and it also provides mental stimulation and stress relief. Play is good for us too. More than anything, your dog wants to spend time with you, and playing together is a perfect opportunity for this. Take the challenge to play at least once a day with your dog for the next month!

IN THE BOXES BELOW, WRITE YOUR START DATE AND WHAT GAME YOU AND YOUR DOG PLAY EACH DAY!

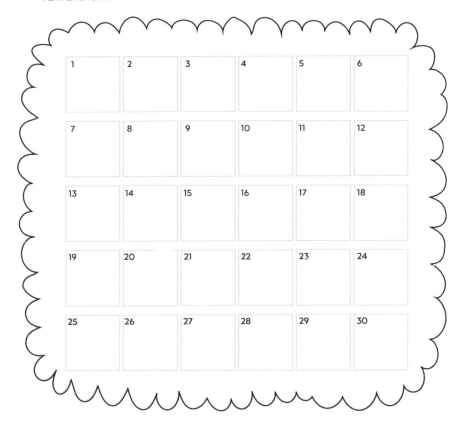

RECALL GAMES

Teaching your dog to come or to "recall" to you isn't just a fun trick, it can literally save your dog's life. This is one of the most important cues you can ever teach your dog, but it can also be a really fun game! The most important thing when playing recall games is not to introduce your verbal cue too early or you risk weakening it, or as some call it "poisoning," by which I mean your dog will not have a clear understanding of what you want when you use your verbal cues. This can happen with any cue/behavior, but it's especially dangerous with something like recall, because your recall can literally be the difference between life and death for your dog if for some reason your leash fails or your dog darts out of your door.

The goal of recall games should always be fun; you want your dog to feel excited and rewarded by being near you. Because of this, it's important never to punish or scold your dog for coming to you.

INSTRUCTIONS

1. Start with high-value treats and reward your dog every time they look at you. Here you are building value in being near and engaging with you.

2. As your dog moves towards you, and when you are sure your dog will come to you (practice this at first in a low-distraction environment like inside your house), use the verbal cue you want to develop: "come," "with me," etc. Whatever you pick, give your dog the treat and praise them.

3. Continue to work in environments where you are sure your dog will come towards you before using the verbal cue, so that you don't accidentally end up telling your dog to do something you don't want, like run in the opposite direction! Gradually

build up your dog's recall by practicing and slowly increasing the level of distraction in the environment.

CATCH ME!

Another fun recall game you can play in a safe area like your fenced yard or inside your house, is to take high-value treats and/or toys (whichever is most valuable to your dog) and move away from your dog as quickly as possible (ideally running), making excited noises and calling "puppy, puppy, puppy," or some other excited phrase that is *not* your recall word or your dog's name—we're just making excited noises because we want our dog to choose to orient itself and come to us, but we don't want to risk misusing a cue since we can't guarantee they will come at this stage. When your dog turns and moves quickly towards you, praise them, and when your dog catches up to you, give them a treat or begin playing with the toy. These high-arousal games will build value for your dog in being near you, and as your dog gets better at the game you can begin introducing your verbal cue for recall!

WHAT LOW-DISTRACTION PLACES CAN YOU PRACTICE RECALL?

_____

_____

When your dog is consistently successful in low-distraction environments, you can start to work in more distractions by bringing your chase/recall game on the road! To keep your dog safe, practice in fully fenced areas or on leash, either a regular six-foot walking leash or a long line.

WHAT ARE SOME HIGHER-DISTRACTION AREAS WHERE YOU CAN PRACTICE?

_____

_____

FIND A PERSON

If you have multiple people living in your home, or people who visit regularly, you can teach your dog to find each person by name!

MAKE A LIST OF PEOPLE WHO LIVE IN YOUR HOUSE OR VISIT REGULARLY:

_____   _____

_____   _____

_____   _____

_____   _____

_____   _____

INSTRUCTIONS

1.   Have each person stand in a circle holding treats.

2.   Point to the person you want your dog to find and say "go find [NAME]!"

3.   Have that person call your dog's name.

4.   Praise and give a treat when the dog approaches.

5.   Have that person repeat the process back to you.

The better your dog gets, the more distance you can add between each person. As your dog gets more experienced, you can also reduce the amount of calling the other person does. Remember to go slowly as you add distance and to work more on your dog finding the other person instead of being called to them. If at any point your dog isn't successful, just go back a few steps, bringing the person closer to you and/or having them call your dog's name. The goal is to always set our dogs up to be successful, so if they ever get stuck, we want to go back to the point where they were able to succeed and then very slowly begin to add in difficulty again after a few successful sessions.

Eventually, after practicing this skill you will be able to send your dog to find anyone in the family, anywhere in the house!

WHO HAVE YOU TAUGHT YOUR DOG THE NAMES OF?

MAGIC TRICKS

Find the cookie in your hand—this game is also a great starter game for teaching your dog to do scent-based tricks and skills. Dogs see the world through their nose, so we certainly aren't teaching them to use their nose, what we're teaching our dogs is that we want to listen to them, that we are paying attention and being thoughtful about what they are telling us. For this reason, I find that scent-based games are a really fun but also really invaluable skill to teach our dogs, because it does so much to foster and build our relationships to our dog.

For this activity all you need are some treats, the smellier the better.

INSTRUCTIONS

1. Put a cookie in one of your hands and show it to your dog without letting your dog have the treat.

2. Close your fist around the treat and close your other fist as well.

3. Hold both hands out to your dog.

4. When your dog paws at or noses at the hand with the cookie, open your hand and give the dog treats and lots of praise!

If your dog paws at the wrong hand, open the hand to show your dog there isn't anything there, then open your other hand, show your dog the treat, and close it again without letting your dog get the treat, and start again. When your dog selects the right hand, give them lots of praise and let them have the treat!

When your dog gets more experienced, you can start to move the cookie between your hands, back and forth, so your dog isn't exactly sure what hand the treat is in. Hold both hands out to your dog to sniff and ask them to select a hand; when your dog gets it right, immediately give them the treat and have a party!

This is a fun "magic trick" that gets your dog's brain going and will also impress your friends!

TREASURE HUNT

It might be a bit of an exaggeration to call this a "treasure hunt," but it's a great way to be a good neighbor. All of us should be carrying poop bags with us when we are out on walks with our dogs, but unfortunately not everyone does. Not scooping after dogs is not only a finable offense in most jurisdictions, but it's also extremely rude. Not picking up after dogs can contribute to the spread of disease, and it also can very easily lead to negative community feelings and perceptions about people with dogs. This can result in parks and other public areas becoming less welcoming to dogs, which isn't something any of us want!

To help improve the overall opinion about dogs in your community, take a treasure-hunt challenge to carry extra poop bags with you and clean up any poop you and your dog come across on your walk! Challenge your other dog-guardian friends to take the challenge and not only clean up after their own dogs but also clean up poop that other people haven't scooped!

HOW MUCH "TREASURE" DID YOU FIND IN A WEEK?

Monday

Tuesday

Wednesday

Thursday

Friday

Saturday

Sunday

TRICK-TRAINING CHALLENGE

Trick training offers you and your dog the opportunity to spend quality time together. Tricks are a fantastic way to build confidence in shy dogs, and a great way to burn off excess energy. There are an unlimited number of tricks that you and your dog can work on together. If you are just getting started with trick training *or* if your dog already knows a lot of tricks, it can be hard to stay motivated with your training. Like with people, if dogs don't practice something regularly, they can easily forget the skill, so it's important to make trick practicing a regular part of your daily life.

For this activity, you can work on tricks your dog already knows but needs more practice at, tricks you want to keep your dog fluent with, or you can teach your dog something completely new and commit to a month of trick training!

INSTRUCTIONS

Pick a new trick to work on each week. This can be a trick that your dog has already been introduced to or something completely new. The key to mastering a new trick in a week is to practice, practice, practice! Try to dedicate a few minutes each day to working on the trick and mark your progress below!

EXTRA CREDIT

Keep working on the previous week's tricks each week to build your dog's skill in even more tricks!

Week 1 trick:

_____

Monday _____
Tuesday _____
Wednesday _____
Thursday _____
Friday _____
Saturday _____
Sunday _____

Week 2 trick:

_____

Monday _____
Tuesday _____
Wednesday _____
Thursday _____
Friday _____
Saturday _____
Sunday _____

Week 3 trick:

_____

Monday _____
Tuesday _____
Wednesday _____
Thursday _____
Friday _____
Saturday _____
Sunday _____

Week 4 trick:

_____

Monday _____
Tuesday _____
Wednesday _____
Thursday _____
Friday _____
Saturday _____
Sunday _____

CHALLENGE REFLECTIONS

HOW DID THE CHALLENGE GO?

_____

_____

_____

WERE THERE TRICKS YOUR DOG STRUGGLED WITH?

WHAT TRICKS WAS YOUR DOG MOST EXCITED ABOUT?

HOLD IT

One of the cutest and most useful tricks if you are trying to get a cute Instagram picture is teach your dog to hold...everything and anything (that is of a safe and appropriate size): everything from their own toys to photo props, sticks you find on your walks, and anything else you might be able to find around the house.

Some dogs are happy to put anything and everything in their mouth, while other dogs are somewhat reluctant to do so. For this trick, the key is to go very slowly, building duration in very small, incremental steps.

INSTRUCTIONS

Start with an object that you would like your dog to hold. I recommend an object that your dog is already happy and comfortable holding—like a toy. If your dog doesn't generally play with toys, then I recommend starting with a hard dog chew or a toilet-paper/paper-towel tube (these tend to be remarkably attractive to a lot of dogs).

1. Show your dog the object you would like them to hold. Initially, praise and treat your dog for any interest in the object, including sniffing, pawing, or otherwise engaging with it.

2. Start upping the criteria by rewarding your dog the instant they put their mouth on the object, then click or verbally mark with praise and treat.

3. After your dog has started to put their mouth onto the object, start to slowly build duration by waiting a fraction of a second longer before clicking/praising and rewarding them. Start to introduce the verbal cue: "take," "hold," and "yours" are a few common terms.

4. Don't be in a hurry to move beyond this stage quickly; we want to be sure that your dog has a solid understanding of the behavior before upping the criteria. As you build more duration with this trick. you can slowly start to remove your hand, at first just for an instant, then return your hand to the object, click/praise, and treat.

5. Continue building duration with your dog's hold skills until your dog is comfortably holding the object. If your dog drops the object or puts it down, do not chastise your dog, just lower the criteria back to a level where they are able to be successful.

Once your dog has hold down, one of the best ways to keep working the skill is to diversify the things you ask your dog to hold. Think about objects of different (safe) weights, and especially objects made of different textures and materials: plastic, fabric, cardboard, metal (this one is often very challenging for dogs). Just make sure that anything you ask your dog to hold isn't going to be dangerous or break in their mouth—some dogs have a very "soft" mouth (a number of breeds, like golden retrievers, were actually bred specifically to have soft mouths for retrieving game without damaging the animals), while other dogs naturally have much harder grips.

TAKE THE THIRTY-DAY HOLD CHALLENGE

HOW MANY THINGS CAN YOU FIND FOR YOUR DOG TO HOLD?
TRY TO FIND SOMETHING NEW EVERY DAY FOR THIRTY DAYS.

1. _____
2. _____
3. _____
4. _____
5. _____
6. _____
7. _____
8. _____
9. _____
10. _____

11. _____
12. _____
13. _____
14. _____
15. _____
16. _____
17. _____
18. _____
19. _____
20. _____

21. _____
22. _____
23. _____
24. _____
25. _____
26. _____
27. _____
28. _____
29. _____
30. _____

CHALLENGE REFLECTIONS

HOW DID THE CHALLENGE GO?

_____

_____

_____

_____

WERE THERE ANY OBJECTS YOUR DOG STRUGGLED WITH?

_____

_____

_____

_____

WHAT OBJECTS WAS YOUR DOG MOST EXCITED TO HOLD?

_____

_____

_____

_____

MY DOG CAN DO MATH!

One of the most impressive and versatile tricks your dog can learn is to find items with a particular scent. You can even teach your dog to find items with your scent. Not only can this be a useful trick, it actually can be something that you can use to "fool" your friends into thinking your dog is a mathematician!

SUPPLIES

- Number blocks
- Plastic or foam numbers—you can usually find these in children's toy sections
- High-value treats

INSTRUCTIONS

1. Take one number and rub it between your hands, put it in front of your dog, and praise and treat them when they explore it. Repeat several times over multiple training sessions. We are teaching our dog to be alert to items with our scent on it.

2. After several sessions, take another number and, using tongs or gloves, place it on the floor, then rub one of the numbers between your hands and put it next to the first number and ask your dog to "search."

3. If your dog alerts to the number that you put down with your scent, give them lots of praise. If your dog alerts to the new number without your scent, just ignore it, take the number with your scent away from the other one, and ask your dog to

search; praise and treat them when they alert to it, and do more repetitions before reintroducing the other numbers.

4. Once your dog is a pro at finding the number with your scent instead of another number, you can add in more (again placing them with tongs or gloves). Once your dog is successful, you're ready for the magic-trick aspect.

5. You can write a simple math problem on a piece of paper, where the answer is the number that you are going to scent. Alternately, you can just verbally state the math problem and then ask your dog to search.

6. Now you're ready to show your friends and family what a math genius your dog is!

HOW DID YOUR DOG DO WITH MATH? WHAT WAS THE RESPONSE TO THIS TRICK?

_____

_____

_____

RED LIGHT/GREEN LIGHT

Practicing "stay" doesn't have to be boring, in fact, the more you make practicing this behavior into a game, the stronger the skill will be for your dog, which for a potentially lifesaving skill like "stay" is very important. This is a great game that you can play with your dog on walks while on leash, or even in your living room. It doesn't take a lot of space to play and is very reinforcing for dogs.

To play the game, you will ask your dog to "wait" and then quickly release your dog to begin moving forward again. For added challenges you can add in toys. I like to think of this as a doggie equivalent to the little kids' game red light/green light.

To start you want to make sure that your dog has a strong "stay" or "wait." If they don't, go back and reinforce/teach that skill first.

QUICK TIPS FOR TEACHING "STAY"

Start by teaching "stay" in a low-distraction environment, for example in your living room. Ask your dog to sit or get down, praise, release (if your dog doesn't have a release word pick one! "Ok" is a common one, but you can select any word you want, you can even pick a different word for each dog), and treat. Start by only asking them to stay for a second at a time, and slowly build up. As your dog gets more familiar with the game, you can add in your "stay" or "wait" verbal cues. As your dog gets more familiar with this skill, you can start to add in more distractions, working the skill (safely on leash) in more distracting areas like your driveway or the park, and adding in other distractions like toys. Just remember to go slowly to keep your dog successful.

GAME

Just like playing red light/ green light as a kid, you cue your dog to wait, praise and treat them, release them to move forward, then repeat.

EXTRA CREDIT

Play the game while asking your dog to do a "standing stay" during this trick, which for most dogs is more challenging than asking the dog to "sit and stay" during the game.

WHERE HAVE YOU PLAYED RED LIGHT/GREEN LIGHT?

WHAT DID YOUR DOG THINK OF THE GAME?

FOUR-ON CHALLENGE

Similar to the two-paws-up challenge, getting your dog to put all four paws up onto something is a fantastic way to build confidence with them. From logs and rocks to small retaining walls and benches, there are so many (safe) places you can ask your dog to get up onto. Getting up and onto objects can help your dog build strength and coordination, and this activity can be high impact.

Be sure that the objects you are asking your dog to get onto are an appropriate height. It's a good idea to look at the American Kennel Club dog agility recommended jump heights for some perspective on safe heights.

- Dogs 11 inches and under at the withers jump 8 inches
- Dogs 14 inches and under at the withers jump 12 inches
- Dogs 18 inches and under at the withers jump 16 inches
- Dogs 22 inches and under at the withers jump 20 inches
- Dogs over 22 inches at the withers jump 24 inches

Check with your vet before asking your dog to do four-on. If your dog is a young puppy—before growth plates have closed, or a senior dog, you will want to avoid four-on. Again, talk with your vet about safety. Also be sure to never ask your dog to jump up and down onto hard surfaces like concrete.

INSTRUCTIONS

1. Begin teaching your dog this trick in a low-distraction environment. Inside your home will be perfect, but equally you can practice this trick in your yard. Make sure to have

some high-value treats on you, and show your dog the object that you want them to get up onto.

2.   Showing your dog the treat in your hand, lead them towards the object while encouraging them to get up onto it.

3.   Once your dog's has gotten up on top of the object, praise/click and treat them.

4.   Practice this several times in a row, and once your dog is able to confidently get up on top of the object every time, start introducing your verbal cue of choice: "Four paws up," "four," and "on top" are all great choices. At first, use the verbal cue as your dog is moving towards the object, right before they get up on top of it.

5.   Once your dog is confident getting onto an object in a low-distraction environment, start to phase out your lure. Keep your high-value treats and ask your dog to get onto an object with your verbal cue. When they do, praise/click and treat them!

6.   Bear in mind that, using this trick, you and your dog can incorporate the environment into your tricks, enriching your walks together, and preparing you both for the sport of parkour, if you're so interested.

TAKE THE CHALLENGE!

You and your dog are ready for the four-on challenge. For the next thirty days, try to find at least one new object each day for your dog to try getting up onto? Don't be afraid to be inventive, just be sure to follow all leash laws and respect private property, monuments, and memorials, and make sure the obstacles you choose are safe for your dog.

1	2	3	4	5	6
7	8	9	10	11	12
13	14	15	16	17	18
19	20	21	22	23	24
25	26	27	28	29	30

CHALLENGE REFLECTIONS

HOW DID THE CHALLENGE GO?

WERE THERE ANY OBJECTS YOUR DOG STRUGGLED WITH?

WHAT OBJECTS WAS YOUR DOG MOST EXCITED ABOUT?

HOW MANY THINGS CHALLENGE

The more training and activities you do with your dog, the more accessories and props you might feel compelled to purchase. While I love dog toys and props as much as the next person, I think being realistic and intentional about what you buy is really important. Our dogs *love* a lot of the things that we purchase for them, but they don't need them. What our dogs care more about than fancy toys and props, is spending time with us. But that doesn't mean we have to be boring.

Pick an object—it can be any size so long as it's safe for your dog (nothing sharp or easily breakable), and try to come up with as many things as you can for your dog to do with or in relationship to the object. Examples: hold; go around it to the right; go around it to the left; go under it; go over it; get onto it with two feet or all four feet; sit while putting their paws onto it, etc. Keep track of all the things your dog can do with an individual object, and when you run out of ideas, pick a new object and keep the game going!

OBJECT: _____

WHAT CAN YOUR DOG DO?

_____

_____

_____

OBJECT: _____

WHAT CAN YOUR DOG DO?

_____

OBJECT: _____

WHAT CAN YOUR DOG DO?

OBJECT: _____

WHAT CAN YOUR DOG DO?

OBJECT: _____

WHAT CAN YOUR DOG DO?

LEARN THEIR NAMES! HOW MANY TOYS CAN YOUR DOG LEARN THE NAMES OF?

If your house is anything like mine, your dog has more than a few toys, but does your dog know the name of each toy? What about their favorites?

To teach your dog the names of toys, I like to start with the toys your dog likes best and begin organically naming and using that name every time you play with your dog: "Get [insert toy name]." Your dog will quickly develop an understanding of that toy's name. To test your dog's understanding, put a toy that they know the name of across the room and ask them to get the toy. If they do, give them huge praise and lots of treats and play with the desired toy. If they don't, it's not a problem, just a sign you need to do more reinforcing of pairing the name of the toy with the item.

When your dog can confidently identify the toy requested across the room, it's time to add in the distraction of other toys. Put the toy near other toys and ask your dog to get the named toy, when your dog does, give them lots of treats and praise. If your dog is distracted or confused by the other toys, ignore them getting the other toy and go find the correct toy and initiate play; that's a sign that you need to back up a little bit with this game and continue to reinforce the name of this toy.

Dogs' minds are incredible, they are able to understand a remarkably large number of words, so you can easily teach your dog the name of all the toys (yes, all those toys) you have! A border collie named Chaser became famous and has been hailed as the smartest dog in the world for this trick. He knows the names of over a thousand toys. Look up videos of him online, it's remarkable! To teach the names of different toys, you'll start the same way as you did with the first toy and slowly start to improve this upon skill by asking your dog to get a named toy in proximity to another named toy. Again, if at any point your dog is confused, go back to the last step where your dog was successful.

YOUR DOG'S TOYS BY NAME:

Description of toy	Name of toy	Dog knows the name?

CHORES

Asking your dog to help out around the house is a fun way to engage with your dog and keep them mentally occupied (not to mention keeping dog toys from taking over your house). One of the easiest chores to get help from your dog with is putting their toys away. I've also found that, for my dogs, a lot of the fun of playing with toys is taking them out of the toy box, and the beauty of putting toys away daily means that tomorrow your dog gets to have a lot of fun taking them out again!

INSTRUCTIONS

1. Start with toys your dog likes, treats, and a toy box or basket where the toys live. Sit with your dog next to the toy box.

2. Give your dog the toy, and while they are still standing over the toy box, hold a treat out to your dog.

3. When they drop the toy, because you have set them up for success, the toy will fall into the bin.

4. Give your dog the treat and offer lots of praise.

5. Repeat, again positioning the toy bin in such a way that your dog will automatically be successful.

6. You can start to integrate the verbal cue you choose: "cleanup," "away," etc.

7. Over time, start to add in a very small amount of distance, inches at a time, until your dog is able to take toys and bring them to the toy box from a distance.

8. You can also start to ask your dog to pick up toys instead of being handed them.

CHORE CHART!

Create a route with your dog and build a routine in which your dog helps by doing some chores (with you) every day of the week! Can you keep things up for a month?

ADD A CHECK MARK OR A STICKER EACH DAY YOU AND YOUR DOG DO CHORES TOGETHER!

MONDAY	TUESDAY	WEDNESDAY	THURSDAY	FRIDAY	SATURDAY
					SUNDAY

MONDAY	TUESDAY	WEDNESDAY	THURSDAY	FRIDAY	SATURDAY
					SUNDAY

MONDAY	TUESDAY	WEDNESDAY	THURSDAY	FRIDAY	SATURDAY
					SUNDAY

MONDAY	TUESDAY	WEDNESDAY	THURSDAY	FRIDAY	SATURDAY
					SUNDAY

Congratulations on your new chore routine! After a successful month of cleaning up together, create a special reward for you and your dog, like a fun outing together or...a new toy!

CUPCAKE-TIN PUZZLE

Keeping your dog mentally exercised is just as important as keeping your dog physically fit. Just like with people, doing puzzles is a great way to stretch your dog's brain. There are a lot of commercially available puzzles on the market, but you don't actually have to spend money to give your dog a lot of mental exercise.

SUPPLIES

- 🦴 A dozen tennis balls
- 🦴 Cupcake baking pan
- 🦴 Treats your dog is excited about

INSTRUCTIONS

Tennis balls fit perfectly into the holes of a standard cupcake tin, so for this game you will put a treat into one or a few of the compartments of the cupcake pan. Then put balls on top of those and into all the rest of the compartments. Show your dog the pan and encourage your dog to search for the treats.

HOW FAST DID YOUR DOG FIND THE TREATS?

_____

WHAT DID YOUR DOG THINK ABOUT THE GAME?

_____

_____

You can play this game repeatedly; just switch what compartments you put the treats in!

SODA-BOTTLE PUZZLE

For this puzzle, your dog will nose at and flip the soda bottles in order to access the treats inside. This puzzle is a great brain game that will keep your dog mentally stimulated. Like with any other puzzle, you want to be sure to supervise your dog while they are playing with this toy.

SUPPLIES

- Wooden dowel
- Between one and three one-liter plastic bottles (depending on the size of your dog)
- Scissors

INSTRUCTIONS

1. Use your scissors to put holes slightly larger than the size of your dowel into the top of the soda bottles.

2. Put the dowel through the holes in the bottle.

3. Take small treats or some of your dog's kibbles and drop them into the bottles.

4. Position the dowel between the legs of chairs making sure that it is stable,

If your dog is really excited about this puzzle, for a more advanced version you can build a wooden stand to hold your soda-bottle holder. This will make the bottles more stable and make it possible for your dog to play this game anywhere in your home.

HOW QUICKLY DID YOUR DOG SOLVE THIS PUZZLE?

_____

_____

_____

_____

NEXT STEPS

GO PLAY!

Congratulations! You and your dog have just completed (up to) a hundred activities, crafts, challenges, and adventures together! I hope that you have both have had a lot of fun, tried something new, found games you love, and explored a little bit more of your world together. Roger Caras famously said, "Dogs are not our whole life, but they make our lives whole," and I couldn't agree more—well except that for some of us our dogs might also be our entire lives. There are so many distractions in our lives, so many things pulling our attention away from what matters most to us—our dogs! It is my hope that through these activities you have found ways to decrease some of those distractions that pull your attention away, and can instead increase the intentional time you spend with your dog.

If you've filled up all the blank pages in this book, congratulations! Now I would like to encourage you to go and purchase a new journal. It can be something fancy you like, or just a simple notebook from the grocery store. The journal itself doesn't matter, what matters are the memories you make and the memories you document inside. Over the years, I have found that recording training goals with my dog, our daily activity, and adventures is extremely helpful for tracking our progress together, and it's a lot of fun! Documenting your activities with your dog can help to motivate you, and your journal will serve as a treasured memory keeper for years to come.

My pups and I hope that this book was just the beginning of the games and adventures you will have and document with your dog!

Sassafras, Mercury, & Sirius

ACKNOWLEDGEMENTS

Thank you to all of the amazing dogs who have been part of my life in the past: Peepers, Snickers, Flash, Sydney, and Cosmo, who were my best friends and helped me develop my passion for working with dogs. I also want to thank my champion trick dog, Charlotte, who completely changed my life and who passed away from cancer while I was writing this book: sweet girl, without you this book would never have been possible. Also, a huge thank you to the dogs I share my home and life with, my retired service dog Mercury, and my giant baby Sirius (trick dog champion, canine good citizen, and trick dog performer) who collaborated in developing and testing all the games, crafts, and activities in this book.

A special thank you to my dog-training beta readers, Kay Pedisich and Morgan Charpentier, who reviewed and gave feedback on earlier versions of this book, and to my patrons, who support my work monthly.

Last and certainly not least, a huge thank you to my partner Kestryl, who is an incredible dog (and cat) co-parent. Thank you for always supporting all of my dog dreams, for supporting our family, baking birthday cakes for me and the dogs, and for spending so much of your free time coming up with and taking us on fun dog-centered adventures!

ABOUT THE AUTHOR

Sassafras Lowrey is a celebrated author and All Star Trainer of the Year, as well as a Certified Trick Dog Instructor (CTDI). Sassafras has been working with dogs for twenty years and has trained and competed in a variety of canine sports including dog agility, rally obedience, canine parkour, and tricks. Sassafras has written regularly for an array of local and national dog- and pet-lifestyle magazines including: *The Bark, Dogster, Whole Dog Journal,* and the *American Kennel Club.* Sassafras has also written about dogs and dog training for the *New York Times,* and has provided expert advice about dogs for AKC TV, BBC, and *Good Housekeeping.*

Sassafras's dog books include the two-time Dog Writers Association of America finalist *Tricks in the City: For Daring Dogs and the Humans that Love Them,* as well as *Bedtime Stories for Rescue Dogs: William to the Rescue* with illustrator Lili Chin, and the lyric-essay collection *Healing/Heeling.* Sassafras and hir dogs spent many years living in New York City, and now live, write, play, and train in Portland, Oregon.

Learn more at www.SassafrasLowrey.com.

Mango Publishing, established in 2014, publishes an eclectic list of books by diverse authors—both new and established voices—on topics ranging from business, personal growth, women's empowerment, LGBTQ studies, health, and spirituality to history, popular culture, time management, decluttering, lifestyle, mental wellness, aging, and sustainable living. We were recently named 2019's #1 fastest growing independent publisher by *Publishers Weekly*. Our success is driven by our main goal, which is to publish high quality books that will entertain readers as well as make a positive difference in their lives.

Our readers are our most important resource; we value your input, suggestions, and ideas. We'd love to hear from you—after all, we are publishing books for you!

Please stay in touch with us and follow us at:

Facebook: Mango Publishing
Twitter: @MangoPublishing
Instagram: @MangoPublishing
LinkedIn: Mango Publishing
Pinterest: Mango Publishing

Sign up for our newsletter at www.mangopublishinggroup.com and receive a free book!

Join us on Mango's journey to reinvent publishing, one book at a time.